Praise for

Puzzle Pieces

In this fascinating book, respected ministry leader Deb Warner takes us on an amazing personal journey of discovery as she unearths forgotten family history that enables her to understand and reclaim her spiritual legacy. This book is part history, part personal family memoir, and part teaching for all of us, as Deb helps us learn how the "saints who have gone before us" impact our lives and destinies today, perhaps much more than we realize. This book will challenge you to look at your own life and ask the question, "God what puzzle pieces are you revealing to show me my spiritual inheritance?"
—Bishop Robert Stearns
Senior Leader, The Tabernacle, Orchard Park, NY

—

Executive Director, Eagles' Wings For so many Pentecostals I have met, the spiritual clock of life begins when and where they first experienced the trans-forming power of the Holy Spirit. What Deb Warner has done is add the biblical theology of "Bethel" that enabled her to map where the Spirit touched three generations of one truly international family.

Every farmer knows the advantage of a three-legged barn stool; it can stand firm on unequal surfaces. Deb's Pentecostal experience is anchored like that three-legged stool. She has learned how to function simultaneously in three time zones with the past as a present memory and the future as a present possibility. She's a living trinitarian movement. She has found the practical spirituality that can stand on the uneven surfaces of life itself.
—Dr. Ray Bakke
Retired chancellor and professor of Global Urban Studies at Bakke Graduate University; Former executive director of International Urban Associates in Chicago, Illinois
Author: *A Theology As Big As the City; The Urban Christian; Street Signs: A New Direction in Urban Ministry; The Expanded Mission of Old First Churches; The Expanded Mission of City Center Churches; Joy At Work: Bible Study Companion; A Surprising Journey: From Saxon to Chicago and Back*

This book will be a blessing to people who need to know their spiritual heritage and their worth and value. It will stimulate hope for the Christian community to search out the spiritual impact of people in their family. Also, the world will know who Deb Warner is—a woman of faith and a spiritual treasure.
—Bishop T. Anthony Bronner
Elim Christian Fellowship, Buffalo, NY
Turning the World Upside Down Covenant Fellowship

—

The Bible is a reflective narrative of ordinary people who had extraordinary visions from God. This author's vision led to a profound ministry discovery. Her passion to uncover, connect and embrace her earthly purpose, as well as her destiny is succinctly captured in *Puzzle Pieces: Discovering My Lost Inheritance*. Referencing the legacy of her great-grand father, Daniel Awrey, Deb creatively weaves her ordinary childhood years, her marriage, missions, motherhood and her ministry into a colorful tapestry. Each event of significance is a *Puzzle Piece*, occurring in phases in different parts of the world, and often without clarity nor interpretation of placement.

The reader is inspired to become reflective in affirming the richness of their God-ordained generational inheritance, acknowledging the faithfulness of the Almighty to bring it to pass.
—Wilma J. Hughey, PhD.
Co-Founder, Faith Temple Community Church, Elmira, NY

—

Pastor Judy and I have known Deb Warner since 1996. She is not only a great friend but a truly gifted minister. Her love and knowledge of the Word of God and her gift of prophecy has enabled her to put into words how she discovered her personal and rightful inheritance. The book is a great read filled with stories, testimonies and illustrations to motivate the reader to unlock the puzzle pieces in their own life so their destiny would be fulfilled. This book will change and inspire you to pursue your inheritance.
Dr Ron & Rev Judy Burgio
Vice President, Elim Fellowship,
Pastor, Love Joy Church, Lancaster, NY

Deb and Al Warner are two of the most amazing people. I first met them about 15 years ago, and I immediately felt a spiritual connection. They were researching Deb's great-grandfather, Daniel Awrey, whom she knew very little about.

She began putting pieces of a puzzle together, and God is still writing the pages of her life as more puzzle pieces are added to her spiritual inheritance. Since that time we first met, Deb has discovered amazing things about Daniel Awrey and her family. It was a legacy she didn't know she had. Just as Deb and her family had lost track of his life and ministry over the last 100+ years, Awrey has been a forgotten pioneer in the history of the Pentecostal movement.

Daniel Awrey was a key leader who came out of Azusa Street. He was good friends with Frank Bartleman, the chronicler of the Azusa Street revival, and many other key figures of the day. Bartleman and Awrey traveled together overseas. The Bartleman family even lived next door to the Awrey family for many years in Los Angeles.

Although he died in Liberia in 1913, Awrey traveled around the world several times and had strong connections with the founders of the Assemblies of God, the Church of God, and the International Pentecostal Holiness Church. You won't want to miss out on the spiritual journey as Deb Warner unlocks the discoveries she made along the way to find her lost generational inheritance.
—Glenn Gohr
Reference Archivist, Flower Pentecostal Heritage Center

—

What a thrilling adventure your book *Puzzle Pieces* opened up to me! The careful, Spirit-led discovery of your heritage of faith, especially the extraordinary life of your great-grandfather Daniel Awrey, serves to validate, clarify, and establish your calling. Now you have made this rich inheritance readily accessible to those who come after you. Even more, you have encouraged each of us to look into our pasts as a way of moving ever forward in the Lord's work. The seeds Daniel Awrey planted in his short life are still bearing fruit more than a century after his death. May we learn from your riveting story that we too have been seeded by others we have never met, and that the seed still in our hands could do Kingdom business long after we are gone.
—Dr. Daniel Woods,
Pastor, Historian, Eden, NC

I once read, "If you don't know where you came from, you don't know what you are about." Today, many people are taking DNA tests hoping to know where they came from. Who are the people in their family ancestry that they never knew? Deb Warner's own story recounts the Puzzle Pieces she discovered in her own family—good, bad and ugly. She tells it all!

Deb's book, *Puzzle Pieces: Recovering Your Lost Generational Inheritance*, stirs a longing inside the reader. This longing will challenge you to discover a lost inheritance in your own family background.

Let Deb Warner challenge you to explore your family history as she shares her own story. Like Deb, you may be surprised at the hidden treasures in your inheritance that you never knew existed!

—Barbara Wentroble
President: International Breakthrough Ministries
President: Breakthrough Business leaders
Author: *Prophetic Intercession; Praying with Authority; Fighting for Your Prophetic Promises; Becoming a Wealth Creator; Council Room of the Lord series: Accessing the Power of God; Accessing Your Prophetic Gift; Accessing God's Healing Glory; Releasing the Voice of the Ekklesia*

—

For well over 20 years now it has been my joy to know and to walk with Al and Deb Warner. Their lives have been a constant testimony to the goodness of God, and the marvel of a couple totally sold out to His plan.

When I first met them decades ago, their passion and personalities reminded me of a random pile of brightly colored puzzle pieces—interesting, intriguing, and delightfully unpredictable!

But as the years unfolded—piece by piece, the magnificent picture came together like a massive jigsaw puzzle revealing the glorious plan that God had all along!

How wonderful that in the midst of all of this Deb discovered a key piece to the puzzle which had been hidden for generations—the mantle of her amazing great-grandfather!

Her pursuit of this family treasure is an inspiration to all of us and may just be the incentive some of us need to investigate our own generational heritages.

—Dennis Wiedrick
Partner with Together International
Over 30 years in ministry—pastoring, teaching, intercession, and extensive overseas missions
Author: *A Royal Priesthood: Reigning With Christ Through Intercession*

Puzzle Pieces

JoAnn,

Embrace your generational inheritance! May your children's children experience the Love you have for God

Joel 1:3 "tell your children"

Blessings!

Deb Warner

Puzzle Pieces

Recovering Your Lost Generational Inheritance

by Deb Warner

Foreword by Bishop Tommy Reid

Puzzle Pieces
Recovering Your Lost Generational Inheritance

© 2020 Deb Warner

Total Fusion Press
PO Box 123
Strasburg, OH 44680
www.totalfusionpress.com

All quotes, unless otherwise noted, are from the New King James Version, copyright 1979, 1980, 1982 by Thomas Nelson, Inc. Used by permission. All rights reserved.
Scriptures marked KJV are taken from The Holy Bible, King James Version, copyright © 1972 by Thomas Nelson, Inc., Camden, New Jersey 08103.

Scriptures marked NLT are taken from the Holy Bible, New Living Translation, copyright © 1996, 2004, 2007, 2013, 2015 by Tyndale House Foundation. Used by permission of Tyndale House Publishers Inc., Carol Stream, Illinois 60188. All rights reserved.

Scriptures marked NIV are taken from the HOLY BIBLE, NEW INTERNATIONAL VERSION, copyright © 1973, 1978, 1984 by International Bible Society. Used by permission of Zondervan Publishing House. All rights reserved.

ISBN: 978-1-943496-19-8

Front cover design: Josh Aul, Nexlevel Design, LLC, www.nexleveldesign.com

Order from:
www.setfreeleaders.com

Published in Association with Total Fusion Ministries, Strasburg, OH
www.totalfusionministries.org

20 21 22 23 24 25 26   7 6 5 4 3 2 1

To my husband, Al, who made this book a joy to put together
and to those who will continue to carry on our family inheritance:
my sons, Caleb and Nathan; Nathan's wife, Megan;
and my grandchildren: Caiden, Gracelyn, and Emersyn

Table of Contents

Foreword...xiii

Acknowledgments xvii

Introduction...xxi

1 – Puzzle Pieces... 1

2 – The Scarecrow 8

3 – Corner Puzzle Pieces... 14

4 – Bones Want to be Remembered.................................. 21

5 – Lost Family Inheritance..31

6 – Where Do I Start?.. 37

7 – A Jubilee Year of Recovery...44

8 – Putting the Puzzle Together 48

9 – Our Visit to Sicily.. 55

10 – There is Power in the Closet......................................61

11 – Generational Blessings 68

12 – The Healing Hug..79

13 – God Sightings..86

14 – Your Legacy...96

15 – Dealing with the Muck.. 103

16 – Funeral Home Visit... 111

17 – Our Generational Bible... 116

18 – The Small Vase.. 119

19 – Curious to Find More 125

20 – Praying For Your Children 130

21 – Your Treasure 142

Appendix: Telling the Lord's Secrets: The Story of Daniel Awrey.........147

Sources For Further Research 163

Foreword
by Bishop Tommy Reid

I DO NOT BELIEVE YOU CAN TRULY understand where you are going without knowing where you came from. Before I can use a map effectively, I must know where I am located on the map. Until I know where I am, I cannot plan where I am going. Much of my life has been built on the memory of my grandmother who received the Baptism in the Holy Spirit in 1907. Although she died before I was born, she became, through the story my mother told me, the spiritual foundational memory on which I would build my life. Her experience of hearing about the Pentecostal awakening and then climbing to the hayloft of the barn for prayer and coming down speaking in tongues became the beginning of my family's spiritual heritage.

I believe our lives are built on the foundation of where we came from. Personally, I have learned that I am not able to see where I am going or set goals for my life without knowing who I am, where I came from, and where I believe God has predestined for me to go.

Deb, the typical Evangelical girl, educated in mainline evangelical schools, had a heritage that she knew nothing about. However, her spiritual journey into becoming a Pentecostal and charismatic leader was already being shaped in her spirit long before she discovered her heritage. God sovereignly created within her spirit, the charismatic leader that she would one day become. Her spiritual inheritance began long before she discovered the contemporary work of the Holy Spirit in the world.

Long after Deb Warner became a Pentecostal, the amazing discovery of where she came from assisted her in also discovering who she really was, where she came from, and where she was going in her future.

This book is the heartwarming and very emotional journey that Deb took in discovering her heritage. Her heritage became the fabric on which God was weaving her future. It is truly an amazing story. Just ask yourself, how would you feel if you found that your great-grandfather, Daniel Awrey had played a major role in the great Pentecostal awakening that swept the earth at the turn of the century? Daniel Awrey was a leader in what we know as one of the greatest revivals in the history of the church.

Although Deb had never seen the demonstration of the Acts 2 experience of speaking in tongues, she discovered that her grandfather had been a major leader in the Pentecostal awakening. And then she discovered that he had received his heavenly language years before the Azusa Street revival and that he was one of the major itinerant evangelists of the Pentecostal revival all over the world.

This amazing story will keep you glued to the pages of this book. Being an evangelical Christian and a denominational missionary, Deb knew nothing about the story of her Pentecostal family and their roles in the history of the church. The day she began to discover the whole story was the day she began to understand the structure and purpose of her life. That is why she called the manuscript "Puzzle Pieces," for suddenly her life began to become a logical sequence of events created by God into a life of destiny and divine purpose.

Personally, I have known Deb for many years, but this book gave me a glimpse into the master artist creating one of his masterpieces. There is in this story the contributing pieces God used in creating a story worthy of becoming a Hollywood theatre extravaganza. A story with great emotion and drama that takes you to Hong Kong, Liberia, Los Angeles, a very small town in Canada, and then all over the world.

May I suggest that you read yourself into this amazing story, for somewhere in your past is woven the wonder of your future. As you see Deb's spiritual inheritance shaping her life even before she knew the story of her family, their unknown history became the foundation on which God would build her life.

So, sit down, light a fire in the fireplace, and get ready to read a story with emotion, intrigue and surprise. In it, you will discover the great artist in heaven who creates the wonder and purpose of our lives. Happy reading....

Tommy Reid
Bishop, Niagara Covenant of Ministries

Acknowledgments

THIS BOOK IS DEDICATED FIRST TO MY husband, Al, who made this book a joy to put together. We dove into stacks of seemingly unrelated family puzzle pieces to find chapter after chapter of the treasures contained herein. What an adventure traveling the world to pursue hidden gifts that generations before us left behind. Even though it has taken years to put this family puzzle together, Al has walked and sometimes run beside me, constantly encouraging me to persevere. His editing made my writing sound much better than I could. Thank you, Al!

I also want to dedicate this book to Glenn Gohr, a great lover of godly history. The first piece I read about my Great-Grandfather Daniel Awrey was Glenn's painstakingly written article which launched me on this journey of surprise and discovery. Glenn was also my final editor. Thank you, Glenn!

I am very thankful for people who poured into my life to make this book happen: Bishop Tommy and Wanda Reid, Dr. Ray Bakke, Ron and Judy Burgio, Dennis and Katie Wiedrick, Dr. Wilma Hughey, Dale and Barbara Wentroble, Bishop T. Anthony Bronner, Pastor Matthew Brown, Bishop Robert Stearns and many others. I'm thankful to those who answered my many questions about family history including my aunts, Esther Brinkley and Grace Munger, Mel Robeck, and Dan Woods.

Who would I be without the godly model and investment of Daniel

Awrey? I dedicate this book to the memory of Daniel Awrey, who has become a spiritual mentor (even though I never met him in person). I have only discovered him through all the wonderful and miraculous events that transpired in his life. Great grandfather Awrey's stories brought me to this point of discovering and claiming my lost spiritual inheritance in order to carry some of the family mantle.

I also honor Daniel Awrey's wife, Ella, my great-grandmother, who endured the hardships of raising five children by herself, once her husband passed away at age 43. She lived a godly life and left a godly legacy through her 101 years of life. I honor my grandmother, Ruth Awrey Smith, who was a stabilizing force throughout my high school years. I also bless my parents, Sam and Marie Smith who grounded my feet in the Word of God, raising me to love God. And even before Daniel and Ella Awrey, generations of people in my family tree who I never knew made an investment in my life and spiritual well-being which prepared the way for me and my family. Thank you to generations that continue to cheer me on from heaven!

A generational inheritance goes on and on, so I dedicate this book to the generations after me: my sons, Caleb and Nathan; my daughter-in-law, Megan; and my grandchildren—Caiden, Gracelyn, Emersyn, and any more grandbabies and great-grandbabies to come. As they continue to claim and carry this godly family inheritance, may they fulfill God's call on their lives!

It has been a great joy to unpack my family stories with my brothers, Dan and David Smith, and see it go on to cousins from New York to Texas to California. We all have been touched and changed by the generations that preceded us.

Thank you, John and Charlotte Cooke, who were my first editors. As I saw the delight and excitement in their eyes, it helped me to stay the long course from starting to completing my first book.

My last and best thank you is reserved for God who "before He made the world … loved us and chose us in Christ to be holy and without fault in His eyes" (Ephesians 1:4 NLT). Before the beginning of time, God wrote the treasure map that I have explored. Thank You, God—may the adventure continue and multiply in every reader!

Introduction

WILL YOU WALK WITH ME ON A journey through a cemetery, a funeral home, an old farm, and a variety of other out-of-the-way places? Actually, we will travel around the world as if it were a gigantic puzzle as we look at snippets of life to discover their meaning.

Imagine the biggest puzzle you have ever seen, complete with a variety of colors and textures. This puzzle in front of us was perfectly designed by the Father for His glory. The mountains and valleys seen in the puzzle will take you through the highs and lows of life. But through it all, each puzzle piece has a divine purpose. Puzzle pieces from one hundred years ago show up as well as pieces that appear to have been created yesterday.

The Bible clearly maps out puzzle pieces for the Christian in Romans 8:28 (NLT): "And we know that God causes everything to work together for the good of those who love God and are called according to his purpose for them."

God exhibited His amazing artistry when He created the world and linked puzzle piece to puzzle piece. What God created is far more intricate than a three-dimensional puzzle. There are so many layers and depths that every time you look, you see a different angle, a new view. It all depends on your perspective. What I see from my perspective, you may not be able to see from your viewpoint.

Have you noticed the recent increased interest in personal genealogy?

It seems like our whole culture is calling out to find their background and family tree. Maybe it is because the Internet has opened up doors of information that were never available before. TV stars do DNA testing to find out their family history and encourage viewers to do the same. But in the bigger picture, perhaps God is stirring up today's generation so that long-lost spiritual inheritance can be recovered.

My hope is that as you read this book, it will not only encourage you to find out information about your ancestors, but more importantly create in you a passion to discover and recover the pieces of the puzzle that God created specifically for you—your BIG PICTURE. You may have the privilege of meeting long lost relatives. You may find that you are related to some famous person. But beyond that, I hope that you will find those generations before you who have prepared the way for your faith journey.

Some of your ancestors have earned spiritual credentials that can transfer to you. **Others along the way have muddied the waters, and it is up to you to filter that bloodline through the blood of Jesus to receive the inheritance that God has custom tailored for you.**

In this process we will talk about scarecrows that have been thrown into your path to keep you from finding your destiny. I hope to create an excitement in you to go treasure hunting and recover a generational inheritance that God has destined you to carry.

> "The Kingdom of Heaven is like a treasure that a man discovered hidden in a field. In his excitement, he hid it again and sold everything he owned to get enough money to buy the field" (Matthew 13:44 NLT).

This investigation is like going into your attic and finding a treasure chest that you never knew you had. At first, it is difficult to open, but finally you open it and find items that make you curious. Some items mean nothing to you at the time and others you immediately understand and lovingly embrace. Some make you laugh and others bring tears to your eyes. Go ahead—run with me on this journey. You will see how I was able to unlock my generational inheritance. Then I will show you steps to unlock your own generational inheritance. You may be richer than you ever knew!

Chapter 1

Puzzle Pieces

Puzzle Pieces. That's what I call them. Over the years, God has dropped puzzle pieces into my lap over and over again. At the time, I did not understand the value and positioning of most of the pieces, but there came the *Aha* moments when my curiosity hit its limit.

Years ago as I was writing in my journal, I felt like I heard the Lord say, "You will carry the mantle of Daniel Awrey." What exactly did that mean? Who was Daniel Awrey?

The only place the puzzle piece would fit was that my great-grandma's last name was Awrey. She was 101 years old when she died, so I had the privilege of having met her when I was young. I went to my dad and asked him, "Who was Daniel Awrey?"

He told me he was my great-grandfather. This aroused my curiosity. I wanted to know more. Dad said people called him a prophet. Awrey traveled around the world encouraging missionaries. That was about all he could tell me. It didn't mean much at the time, so I put the puzzle piece in my pocket and went on with life.

A few years later, my husband, Al, and I met in college. We went to

Peru with a college winterim class, and we fell in love with the country and with each other. The trip confirmed our desire and call to follow God as foreign missionaries, specifically to Peru, South America.

Preparation was important to our denomination. For the first step, we both graduated from college. Step number two had us pastoring a church near Poughkeepsie, NY, for six years. The congregation became our family. We could have spent our entire life in that beautiful community with such wonderful people. But we had a greater "Call." Not just our Jerusalem, but also "the ends of the earth." Could that have been a God-given generational inheritance calling from my past?

In preparatory step number three, the mission board encouraged my husband to complete his Master's degree before we went to the mission field. We headed to Chicago where Al studied at Northern Baptist Theological Seminary under his mentor, Dr. Ray Bakke. We interned in a Puerto Rican church while I taught in an inner-city Christian school to help pay the bills. My class was made up of 17 fourth grade students: 14 Puerto Rican,

AL, DEB & CALEB WARNER
SERVING IN
Hong Kong

1 Mexican, 1 white, and 1 black. I learned a lot of Spanish that year, realizing that I was preparing to go as a missionary to a Spanish-speaking country.

After Al completed his degree in Urbanology (the study of how cities work), we met with the mission board again as we made final preparations to leave for our overseas assignment. At the meeting, they let us know they were no longer sending missionaries to work in Peru. The national church was mature and was taking over the work that missionaries had previously done. They asked if we would consider going to Hong Kong instead???

Hong Kong? Hong Kong? I wasn't even sure where it was. The men left the room to give Al and me the opportunity to discuss this drastic change. We looked at the huge world map on the wall. Where exactly was Hong Kong? Al found it. We believed that these men must know what they were offering us. Didn't they hear God for us? With so little information and lots of blind faith, we agreed to go to Hong Kong.

Was I unknowingly being pulled toward my generational inheritance? Was there an unknown mantle I was meant to carry? I didn't recognize or consider any of this at the time.

We arrived in Hong Kong in 1986 with our three-year-old son, Caleb. We felt overwhelmed with the change in language and culture compared to the Puerto Ricans that we had grown to love. The study of the Cantonese language was a daunting challenge compared to Spanish. The music in Chinese church was much more traditional. We were painfully stretched.

On the plus side, we loved the city life with no need for a car because of the amazing transportation system. We slowly adjusted and eventually found ourselves loving our new friends in Hong Kong as family.

Although language school was difficult, we pursued the call to fulfill the destiny that we felt upon us. Still unbeknownst to me, that generational inheritance kept calling. Four months after arriving, we were surprised to find out that I was pregnant with a second son. We had only planned to have one child so this was a major adjustment to work through for both of us, especially with the rigors of language school. Although we felt unprepared, we understood that God orders our steps and we knew that this son was somehow very special. Nathan arrived three-and-one-half weeks early, healthy and full of life.

DIVINE SURPRISE ALERT! My paternal grandmother lived in California. I spent most of my growing up years in New York State, but

during my high school years we lived near my family in California. Those three years gave me opportunity to know my grandmother better.

After the birth of Nathan, I received a letter from my grandmother. She asked if I knew that she had lived in Hong Kong as a child. Did I know that her younger brother, John, was also born in Hong Kong? Did I know that her brother, David, died as a child and was buried in Shanghai?

No one was more shocked at this news than me. Could it be that God had charted my path as a missionary to Hong Kong to recover a generational inheritance? This was a new beginning to explore my generational call.

I was surprised by the history of having birthed a son in the same place my Great-grandfather Daniel Awrey had birthed a son nearly one hundred years earlier. However, as a young mother living overseas, struggling to learn a new language and culture, I didn't have much time to focus on my grandmother's letter. It was just another puzzle piece that didn't fit. I was still years away from finding out who this man, Daniel Awrey, really was.

After my son was born, I began to experience health issues that caused continuous infections, pain, and exhaustion. Following much prayer and counsel, we decided it was best to return home to the States. We pursued medical help, taking a break from the stress of ministry in order for me to heal. After a year, my doctors gave me a clean bill of health. We moved to Western New York in 1989 to plant an evangelical church.

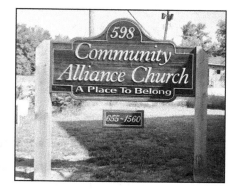

Being back in ministry was wonderful. Once again we fell in love with the community and the people God brought to us. A few years into our pastorate, a key couple from our small church went to Toronto to attend special meetings at the Toronto Airport

Christian Fellowship. This was the place where the "Toronto Blessing" was taking place. This move of God was focused on the outpouring of the love of the Father.

Our friends offered to pay our way if we wanted to go. We accepted out of curiosity but with some reluctance. We had heard enough about the meetings to wonder if they would fit into our spiritual "boxes." This was unfamiliar territory to us.

After attending a meeting, we waited in line to be prayed for, not sure what to expect. We were hesitant. A young teenage girl came up to pray for Al. She looked up at him and asked, "Are you a pastor?"

"Yes," my husband responded.

She continued, "I believe you are giving out of the last drops from the bottom of your bucket. But God wants to fill you so full that others will receive from the splash of your overflow."

That was it. Al dropped to the floor and rested in the Father's arms for several hours. He finally awoke when the cleaning person began running the vacuum cleaner.

How might God introduce you to your generational inheritance when it doesn't fit into your boxes? Might He release something unfamiliar to you? Then you touch it. You examine it. You look at it from all angles. You pray over it. You might even set it down for a while. Then would you ask, "Is this God?" We did all that and more. Something happened to us that we couldn't explain. But we left that meeting with more peace than we had experienced in years. Were we beginning to tap into an inheritance from a past generation?

From that experience we had a new understanding of the vision that God gave Peter in which He commanded Peter to eat something that his religion declared was unclean.

"The next day as Cornelius's messengers were nearing the town, Peter went up on the flat roof to pray. It was about noon, and he was hungry. But while a meal was being prepared, he fell into a trance. He saw the sky open, and something like a large sheet was let down by its four corners. In the sheet were all sorts of animals, reptiles, and birds. Then a voice said to him, 'Get up, Peter; kill and eat them.'

'No, Lord,' Peter declared. 'I have never eaten anything that our Jewish laws have declared impure and unclean.' But the voice spoke again: 'Do not call something unclean if God has made it clean.' The same vision was repeated three times. Then the sheet was suddenly pulled up to heaven. Peter was very perplexed. What could the vision mean?" (Acts 10:9-17 NLT).

Like Peter, we had to work through what God was trying to tell us through this whole experience. Some of our Christian friends considered these manifestations "unclean." It took time and internal struggle to wrestle through our experiences in Toronto. But God was ordering our steps and leading us down an unfamiliar path that was both fascinating and terrifying.

Chapter 2

The Scarecrow

YEARS AGO, GOD TOLD US THAT WHEREVER we go our presence would change the atmosphere. He let us know that we would not know how different the situation might have been without our presence.

I remember times my husband and I would attend a church service and all kinds of uncommon things (at least unfamiliar to us) would happen. We could have wondered what kind of church has these things happening? Or we could ponder whether our presence, carrying our calling and anointing, may have influenced the "normal" of that church service.

John Paul Jackson writes, "Everywhere we set our feet, we are bringing the light of God to that place, and the enemy has to formulate a response to our presence. When we move to a city, country, state, area or province, the enemy cannot continue on his normal course. He must react to our presence, and he must also react to the way the Earth responds to our presence. As it was created to do, the land recognizes the light of God within us, and it responds to that light. Creation longs for God and His presence and whatever would reveal a true statement of His nature." ("The Unstoppable Power of God's Light by John Paul Jackson," https://www.patheos.com/blogs/robertricciardelli/ ricciardelli/the-unstoppable-power-of-gods-light-by-john-paul-jackson/)

What does that mean for you? Could it be that the atmosphere in the spirit realm recognized you when you arrived at your assignment? Perhaps you carried a generational assignment from the spiritual DNA of a relative who had started that assignment. Jesus' cousin, John the Baptist, prepared the way for Jesus. Who might have prepared the way for you?

Creation itself is longing, waiting, and watching for us to rise up and be who God has called us to be.

"For the creation waits in eager expectation for the children of God to be revealed" (Romans 8:19 NIV).

What authority do you walk in? What spiritual credentials do you have? Do you even know? The enemy works overtime to keep you from realizing your potential in Christ.

When a farmer is planting a crop, he often raises up a scarecrow. His goal is to scare off birds and other predators before they can steal his treasure, his precious produce. What treasures have you run away from because of scarecrows put up by the enemy?

I believe if you really knew who you were, or knew the potential of whom God created you to be, you would live very differently. What inheritance is in your bloodlines? What is God's design for you to change your world? What is the rich deposit inside you that has been passed down from generation to generation?

"'But for you who fear my name, the Sun of Righteousness will rise with healing in his wings. And you will go free, leaping with joy like calves let out to pasture. On the day when I act, you will tread upon the wicked as if they were dust under your feet,' says the Lord of Heaven's Armies" (Malachi 4:2-3 NLT).

Could there be a treasure hidden in your past? Could there be a generational inheritance that you have never uncovered? Could there be a gold mine that you have never found? Look at the Old Testament. It is a historic book specifically naming people in the family tree coming down from Adam.

The Bible faithfully records the good, the bad, and the ugly. We are introduced to Noah who gave his life and future to God, trusting that he would see his family saved. His obedience spared the human race. The Lord typically introduces Himself as the God of Abraham, Isaac, and Jacob. We meet people like David who won many a battle for the Kingdom, but had a relationship with Bathsheba that exposed his personal flaws. My belief is that all of us have a divine call on our lives, but the enemy will do whatever he can to keep that from being fulfilled.

Years ago my mother-in-law was doing a family tree. She wanted to  know about the history of my family so that she could include it. I respectfully told her that she didn't want to hear about my family. The shame of my grandfather's (the son-in-law of Daniel Awrey) life was heavy on our family. From what we had been told by my dad, his father had been a pastor who left God, left his family, and claimed to have broken all of the Ten Commandments before he died in a prison in Texas.

I remember traveling to Texas as a child, walking through a burr-infested cemetery looking for my grandfather's gravestone. The pain of the family was so great that no one had even purchased a gravestone for him. Before we left, my dad ordered a gravestone for his father.

Because of the painful experiences of my dad's childhood, he never spoke about his upbringing. He moved our family from California to New York State to give us a fresh start. Every five years we traveled to California to visit my Grandma Smith, my Great-grandma Awrey, my Great Aunt Ina, my Great Uncle John, my father's two sisters and one cousin. They were mostly strangers to me. Little did I recognize the hidden treasure that was in my genes. The enemy had successfully erected a scarecrow two generations ago—my grandfather— to keep me from finding the spiritual inheritance that was mine from three generations ago—my great-grand-father, Daniel Awrey.

James Goll encourages us to research our foundations: "Asking great questions leads to finding great answers. Probe into the roots of your heritage with questions like: What is my family's history, ethnic background, religious heritage, and so on?

Researching your foundations can help you know how to build properly and what potential opportunities may exist for personal growth and development. Study to show yourself approved. Research the question: What does my name mean? Then redemptively turn your name into a promise as a tool of discovering your prophetic destiny. Claim your generational inheritance and call forth blessing. Remember, the power of a blessing is greater than the power of a curse." (James W. Goll, "How to Grow in Divine Revelation," http://www.elijahlist.com/words/display_word.html?ID=14896)

Let me remind you of Exodus 20:5-6 (NLT): "… for I, the Lord your God, am a jealous God who will not tolerate your affection for any other gods. I lay the sins of the parents upon their children; the entire family is affected—even children in the third and fourth generations of those who reject me. But I lavish unfailing love for a thousand generations on those who love me and obey my commands."

That means that the generational blessings of God are two hundred and fifty times more powerful than the generational curses—a thousand generations for those who love God.

As you read this book, you will hear the joys and the pains of recovering a generational inheritance. Sometimes when looking for a treasure, one must go into dark caves and initiate uncomfortable conversations. Other times God allows amazing and supernatural surprises as you dig through the muck. You will hear stories of both. Certain painful stories I uncovered, I have chosen not to repeat in their entirety. Some things are better left unsaid. But the joys have far outweighed the pain.

Come walk with me through the wandering journey as I have pursued my God calling. My hope is that you will be challenged to fight through the scarecrows that the enemy has erected so that you may uncover and recover the treasures that the Father has hidden under those scarecrows.

My good friend, Pastor Matthew Brown, preached a sermon on the scarecrows in our lives. He referred to them as "Goliaths." He said, "Find Goliath and you will find your future. God's got a next when I deal with my now." Come away with a new perspective, a heavenly perspective. David's perspective was different than King Saul's. Saul saw Goliath as too big to beat. David, viewing Goliath from God's perspective, saw him as too big to miss. Adjust your viewpoint on your family inheritance and you will adjust the spiritual authority with which you walk.

Generations before you have already paid the price with their blood, sweat, prayers and tears to allow you to be where you should be. There is no need for you to pay the price again. Pastor Brown gave a thought-provoking fact. Goliath's name means "uncovered." As David answered the call to fight and kill Goliath, the toppling of a giant "uncovered" the truth of God's word, transforming the army of Israel from fear-filled cowards to faith-filled warriors. When the army of Israel grabbed hold of God's perspective, they won the battle.

Doug Addison, a prophetic speaker, author and coach, released a word, "Ancient doors and gates are callings and gifts that have been given to your ancestral or generational line. These represent inheritances that God intended for you and your family but were stopped or delayed for a number of reasons. Don't be intimidated. When God showed me the ancient doors and heavenly gates from Psalm 24:7, I saw what looked like a scene out of the Indiana Jones movies. Whenever Indiana Jones was about to recover a lost treasure, there were always obstacles that he had to overcome. As these ancient, Heavenly doors and gates start to open, it will expose some cobwebs (old thinking), spiders (demonic distraction) and creepy crawlers that have collected around the doors. Don't be scared of them. As you move forward, God is there to get you through."

So don't be intimidated! God has a spiritual and physical inheritance for you to find and recover. Rip down your scarecrow. Kill your Goliath so you can get on to your next assignment!

Chapter 3

Corner Puzzle Pieces

Have you ever met someone and had no idea how important that person would be to your future? I am calling these people "corner pieces" to our puzzle. When we were pastoring, we connected with Bishop Tommy and Wanda Reid, a highly respected pastoral couple in a neighboring town and

pastors of the Full Gospel Tabernacle (The Tab) in Orchard Park, NY. We asked them for wisdom in dealing with issues in our community.

My husband began to regularly meet with the pastor. I decided to meet with his wife as I dealt with personal issues in my life. I also needed help in understanding some new-to-me spiritual manifestations happening in our church. Al and I were blessed as our relationship grew with Bishop Tommy and Wanda, our corner puzzle pieces. They made us feel safe and began to bring order to the outline of our dramatically shifting puzzle. They not only understood, but also helped us to understand and walk out the Charismatic element that had been introduced into our lives and ministry in Toronto.

My hunger for God was growing and I began to "sneak" over to attend

Wanda's Bible study, even though we were pastoring our own church. Wanda and the women welcomed and loved me as though I was one of their church members. Wanda told me how "renewal" had come to the Tabernacle. We began attending special renewal services at The Tab on Sunday and Wednesday nights. We felt the overwhelming presence of God as never before.

God was doing a work in us that we didn't see or fully understand at the time. He was slowly introducing Himself to us as a Charismatic and supernatural God. He was blowing up our religious boxes. It was definitely the personal love from the Reids, this father and mother of the faith, that helped us embrace a previously unfamiliar and uncomfortable walk.

We began to understand the meaning of a prophetic word as we attended a conference in Watertown, NY, in October, 2006, where Chuck Pierce, an internationally recognized prophet was speaking. On October 9th Chuck gave a word that intrigued us. "You will know when God is ready to move when you see the 'tops of the trees break off.' Mark this year where the floods are."

What could this mean? The word took on a fresh significance for us when Thursday night, October 12th (three days later), two feet of snow fell in Buffalo! This early snowfall was dubbed the "October Surprise." Since there were still leaves on the trees, the branches collected the snow and began to snap and crash to the ground. The "tops of the trees began to break off " in Buffalo. The temperature dropped and a flood watch was issued when the snow began to melt!

Something was happening in Buffalo and it certainly didn't feel good to us! We were stuck in our home for days with no electricity. Even when our electricity came back on, there were trees covering our streets and nowhere to go. Could God use this storm to trap me at home to shake up the puzzle pieces again?

With no place to go, I was bored. For some reason (God?), I called my brother, Dan in Wheaton, IL, and asked him what he knew about his namesake, our great-grandfather, Daniel Awrey. My brother referred me to what he had read on the Internet. Suddenly my search for my inheritance was alive again. What I was about to discover would change my life forever.

I googled "Daniel Awrey." I quickly discovered that my Great-grandfather Daniel Awrey spoke in tongues in 1891 and my Great-grandmother Ella Awrey spoke in tongues in 1897. What??? I grew up in a preacher's home and had never heard anyone speak in tongues until my high school years in California. Why had the enemy worked so hard to hide this part of my family tree? Did the scarecrow of my grandfather's moral failure conceal some kind of treasure from me?

With a new sense of anticipation, I continued searching the Internet. I read an article by Glenn Gohr (a Reference Archivist at the Flower Pentecostal Heritage Center) that began answering my many questions. As Glenn would later tell me, a clergyman who wore a clerical collar and kept showing up in old photographs intrigued him. It turned out to be my Great-grandfather Daniel Awrey, my Grandma Smith's father. After much research, Glenn wrote the Daniel Awrey piece for the *Assemblies of God Heritage* magazine that was printed in the Winter of 2000-01. It took me five years and an October surprise snowstorm to catch up with this huge chunk of my inheritance. (The article in its entirety can be found in the appendix of this book).

As I read, I caught glimpses of my great-grandfather. Daniel Awrey spoke in tongues in 1891, a few years before the Azusa St. Revival in Los Angeles. (Note: from my evangelical upbringing, I had never heard of the Holy Spirit outpouring at Azusa Street.) He traveled around the U.S. sharing and teaching this Pentecostal message. When he heard about the Azusa Street revival, he headed to California in 1906. Because of his early experiences, he was viewed as a fatherly figure at Azusa Street. He was invited to

speak and bring wisdom to the spiritually hungry crowds.

His heart was so moved that from 1909-1913, he traveled around the world three and one half times, ministering on five continents. He was privileged to speak at the Sunderland convention in England three consecutive years alongside other well-known speakers such as Smith Wigglesworth. He traveled with Frank Bartleman, the chronicler of the Azusa Street Revival.

Daniel Awrey's name is found in the founding documents of three denominations: the Church of God (Cleveland, Tennessee); the Assemblies of God; and the International Pentecostal Holiness Church. On his final overseas trip, he traveled to Liberia, West Africa. After only six weeks, he died of malaria and is buried there. (My husband presented a major paper on Daniel Awrey at the Society for Pentecostal Studies, meeting in Lakeland, FL in 2015. This has helped me to continue to dig for more.)

Let's get back to the puzzle pieces the Reids helped us to assemble. By 2006, after twenty years of pastoring, Al and I had left full-time pastoring to start Set Free Inc., our own non-profit organization. (More on that later.) We were attending Pastor Tommy and Wanda Reid's church, The Tab, an Assemblies of God church in Orchard Park, a suburb of Buffalo, NY.

The Tab was celebrating an anniversary with a special commemoration service. I brought a copy of Glenn Gohr's article to show Bishop Tommy Reid, sharing what I had just found out about my Great-grandfather. He quickly skimmed the article. His eyes widened.

"Do you know who these people are in this article?"

"No," I responded. I had never heard of Frank Bartleman, Howard Goss, A. A. Boddy, T. B. Barratt, B. H. Irwin, or many other leaders spoken about in the article. I had been raised in an evangelical home and these were prominent Pentecostal names. Pastor Reid invited me to come to the pulpit and share my newly-discovered Pentecostal heritage. That night I

became a celebrity in my home church.

I began this chapter talking about the importance of corner puzzle pieces. As I write this in 2019, my husband, Al has co-authored two books with Tommy Reid, *Create Wealth to Build God's Dream* and *Radical Revolution*. Ask God to remind you of a time when you met a person, but were clueless as to how important they would be to understanding and assembling your puzzle. Bishop Tommy and Wanda Reid have been corner pieces for us.

So let's keep journeying together as we uncover our generational treasure. So far, my search has taken me:

- north to Mimosa, Ontario, Canada
- west to Azusa Street, Los Angeles, California
- west to Springfield, Missouri
- south to Falcon, North Carolina
- south to Cleveland, Tennessee
- far East to Hong Kong
- southwest to Denton, Texas
- a world away to Liberia, West Africa
- and across the ocean to Italy.

I would love to share the joys and disappointments along the way to encourage you to dig deep and pick up your own generational inheritance. Explore your family tree. Dig deep to examine your roots. Pick up everything that you were meant to carry to turn the world upside down for Christ.

Chapter 4

Bones Want to be Remembered

CEMETERIES ARE AMAZING PLACES. YOUR EYES CAN be drawn to the huge monuments towering over certain graves? What is their story? Why people spend so much money on a monument when they would not even be alive to view the stone? They <u>want to be remembered</u>!

Look at these verses from the Old Testament:

> "But watch out! Be careful never to forget what you yourself have seen. Do not let these memories escape from your mind as long as you live! And be sure to pass them on to your children and grandchildren" (Deuteronomy 4:9 NLT).

> "And you must commit yourselves wholeheartedly to these commands that I am giving you today. Repeat them again and again to your children. Talk about them when you are at home and when you are on the road, when you are going to bed and when you are getting up" (Deuteronomy 6:6-7 NLT).

Tombstones tell us that dead people <u>want to be remembered</u>. In the Book of Genesis, Joseph wanted to be remembered. He wanted generations after him to receive the inheritance that was promised to his family when Abraham, his great-grandfather, was alive.

"The Lord had said to Abram, 'Leave your native country, your relatives, and your father's family, and go to the land that I will show you. I will make you into a great nation. I will bless you and make you famous, and you will be a blessing to others. I will bless those who bless you and curse those who treat you with contempt. All the families on earth will be blessed through you'" (Genesis 12:1-3 NLT).

"Then the Lord appeared to Abram and said, 'I will give this land to your descendants.' And Abram built an altar there and dedicated it to the Lord, who had appeared to him" (Genesis 12:7 NLT).

God made a promise to Abraham that his descendants would be given the land where he stood. God promised it to him. Joseph was privileged to be born in that land of promise. But God allowed Joseph to be sold into slavery which took him to Egypt, far from the land of promise.

As impossible as this seems, all this was by divine design. God used Joseph to rescue not only his family, but also the nation of Israel from starvation. Even in Egypt, Joseph remembered his homeland. He understood the promise that God gave to Abraham about that land of promise. Joseph <u>wanted his people to remember and to return to the land to receive the promise.</u>

So Joseph made the Israelites swear an oath in Genesis 50:25-26 (NLT): "Then Joseph made the sons of Israel swear an oath, and he said, 'When God comes to help you and lead you back, you must take my bones with you.' So Joseph died at the age of 110. The Egyptians embalmed him, and his body was placed in a coffin in Egypt."

There was a generational inheritance just waiting for the Israelites when they returned to this land of promise. Joseph ensured that God's people would return to get their inheritance, guaranteeing that <u>they would be remembered.</u>

Here is the follow up:

> "Moses took the bones of Joseph with him, for Joseph had made the sons of Israel swear to do this. He said, 'God will certainly come to help you. When he does, you must take my bones with you from this place'" (Exodus 13:19 NLT).

Picture this—Joseph's bones were carried through the Red Sea. The bones were sitting there when the Ten Commandments were given to Moses on Mount Sinai. For forty years, they were transported through the Wilderness. In all, Joseph's bones waited 400 years before being taken to the promised land. Imagine a child 20 years into the journey in the wilderness asking his or her parent, "What's in the box?" Even the box carried the hope that <u>the bones of Joseph would be remembered</u>. Finally ...

> "The bones of Joseph, which the Israelites had brought along with them when they left Egypt, were buried at Shechem, in the plot of land Jacob had bought from the sons of Hamor for 100 pieces of silver. This land was located in the territory allotted to the descendants of Joseph" (Joshua 24:32 NLT).

Joseph grasped a generational God—the God of Abraham, Isaac, and Jacob. What generational inheritance is waiting to be picked up by you?

All the promises that were made to Abraham were fulfilled according to Joshua 21:43-45 (NLT): "So the Lord gave to Israel all the land he had sworn to give their ancestors, and they took possession of it and settled there. And the Lord gave them rest on every side, just as he had solemnly promised their ancestors. None of their enemies could stand against them, for the Lord helped them conquer all their enemies. Not a single one of all the good promises the Lord had given to the family of Israel was left unfulfilled; everything he had spoken came true."

All it takes to lose it all is for one generation to fail to transfer its

beliefs and principles to the next generation. Christianity is always one generation
from either extinction or multiplication.

> "After that generation died, anoth-
> er generation grew up who did not
> acknowledge the Lord or remember
> the mighty things he had done for
> Israel" (Judges 2:10 NLT).

I truly do not want to be the weak link
in the chain that causes the generational
inheritance to be lost. But even more, I
want the generation that follows me to
grab hold of the promises and blessings for
which I have worked so hard. The late Bob

Jones, a well-recognized prophet, prophesied over us that his ceiling would
be our floor. I want my children to start off stronger, accelerate faster, to
stand taller on my shoulders. Lance Wallnau calls it, "The Believer's Edge!"

Our plans to recover what had been lost continued. We drove to Mimosa, Ontario (60 miles northwest of Toronto) where Daniel Awrey was born.
We were not sure exactly what we were looking for or what, if anything,
we would find. Actually, the town of Mimosa does not even exist anymore,
but Erin Township does. In my devotions that morning, God said, "You
are loved. Enjoy today's surprises—I've tucked them in for you."

As Al was preparing for the trip, he found pictures on-line of gravestones with the Awrey name. As we headed there, we recognized we were
in unknown territory, but we believed God would direct our steps. Our
GPS brought us to dirt roads and THEN WENT BLANK! Apparently,
the satellites could take us no farther.

Where was this cemetery? It's always best to check with the locals when looking for old cemeteries. In spite of my hesitancy, Al pulled into a drive-way with a sign that read, "Hidden Meadow Farm." It was a beautiful horse farm with chickens, pigs, and more. The farm included barking dogs that made me stay in the car while Al knocked on the door. No one was home ...

We checked out another house where a man was working in the drive-way. Al told him that my great-grandfather had been born nearby and asked if he knew of any local cemeteries. With his directions, we continued on our trek. The first and second cemeteries we went to both had "Awrey" gravestones. We excitedly took pictures to add to our historical journal.

We took a break for lunch. We went to a newly opened (<u>only three days before</u>) restaurant called, "The Coach House Creamery." It was obviously an old building that had been remodeled, but the outside was still the same ... an old Coach House where travelers would catch the stagecoach. Remember, Daniel Awrey became a world traveler from this place. Inside the restaurant was an enlarged mural on the wall of

that same street in 1910, just how Daniel Awrey would have seen it over one hundred years ago. Remember this restaurant had only been <u>open three days</u>! What a surprising puzzle piece! We saw Daniel Awrey's world.

Are there moments when time present connects with time past? In God there is no limit to time—timelessness, eternity. As I stood there, I sud-denly was dizzy and took a step backwards. I decided to sit down. Could it be that I stepped back in time? Could this be the same building where Daniel Awrey stood over 100 years before as he left by stagecoach on his

"around the world" adventures??? I can't know for certain, but I do know God orders our steps so we can find those hidden treasures!

After lunch, we headed to the Wellington County Museum and Archives, a regional museum. We uncovered more family history including:

1) We found the Awrey family lived in France, but moved to Ireland. Their name at that point was L'Aurient. As they sailed to the U.S. across the ocean, all of the family got sick and died with the exception of one son. A German family took in this young son. They found his name difficult to pronounce so they changed it to "Awrey." This was significant to me because it meant that everyone with the Awrey surname is somehow related to me.

2) The family came from Ireland to New Jersey (1812), but since they were Loyalists to the British throne, when the War of 1812 broke out, they relocated to Niagara Falls, Ontario and eventually to Mimosa, Ontario. With Canada still owned by the British, they were on the safe side, the Loyalist side, of the battle lines.

3) The Wellington County Museum archivist found maps of land that showed where George Awrey (Daniel's father) owned two 100-acre lots. He had given a portion of his land for a school, the Awrey School #9.

We left the museum to check out the "family farm." You will never guess where it was?!? **HIDDEN MEADOW FARM**—<u>Our very first stop</u>! We had a great laugh knowing this was another of the surprises from the Father that He had promised me that morning in my devotions.

We went in search of the Awrey school building. It still stood and looked exactly like the pictures from more than a century before. A couple was living in it. We explained our family story. Although friendly, they were opposed to us coming inside, which we understood. The gentleman said the chalkboards were still on the walls from the time it was a school.

Time to return to Hidden Meadow Farm. This time our knock on the front door introduced us to Geoff and Brenda Pantling, the owners for the last 30 years. Our adventure continued as we talked and talked about the history of the land, walking with Geoff through the old barn filled with harvest (hay), which was built by George Awrey (Daniel Awrey's father) around 1880.

Geoff and Brenda were as excited to share their stories with us as we were with them. They then gave us the abundance from their farm (a portion of my generational inheritance)—fresh eggs, farm-raised bacon, homemade maple syrup (from the trees on the land), and a barn door hinge from 1883. We plan to have the hinge framed. Oh the stories that hinge could tell …

The barn door hinge gave way to a bigger discussion—could God be opening wide the doors from our past to make a difference in our present and future? "Fling wide you heavenly gates"—the doors of harvest are wide open! We loved following the treasure map to our previously hidden heritage.

But that's not the end. The Pantlings invited us to join them for Canadian Thanksgiving in October to meet some of our long lost, distant relatives. We did. It was extraordinary to meet extended family and exchange stories with strangers who quickly became part of our family tree.

What happened to the generations who lived previous to us? Set before you is a baton. As you reach for and grasp the baton, know that others went before you to prepare the way. That baton is stained with the blood, sweat, and tears shed to establish a godly generational inheritance. These champions who gave their lives for the Kingdom want and need to be remembered. They are filling the heavenly grandstands, cheering you on for your leg of the race!

A quote from Lance Wallnau (a significant teacher on the seven mountains of influence) captures the essence of this scene:

"Recognize that the story is bigger than yourself. You are destined to be alive now. There is a pulsating recognition within each of us. We have a sense that God is doing something now and we know we're meant to be a part of it. You play a critical role in the harvest of souls. **Destiny is not about you, but rather a purpose God has positioned you for that is bigger than yourself.** You are entering into and inheriting a six thousand year labor of prophets, martyrs, reformers and missionaries who came before you."

You have more influence than you know!

Do you want to expand your world, influence those around you, leave an inheritance that continues to grow? You've been handed the baton ... what will you do with it?

"Repeat them again and again to your children. Talk about them when you are at home and when you are on the road, when you are going to bed and when you are getting up. Tie them to your hands and wear them on your forehead as reminders. Write them on the doorposts of your house and on your gates" (Deuteronomy 6: 7-9 NLT).

In your family tree, what bones may be waiting to be remembered? What is that in your hands? Will you pass on a cleaner, more sanctified baton to the next generation than was handed to you? It is your leg of the race. RUN WELL!

Chapter 5

Lost Family Inheritance

ON ANOTHER VENTURE, WE HEADED BACK TO the farm in North Syracuse, NY where I was raised. My mother's parents, Grandpa and Grandma Buda, came from Sicily to Syracuse. Grandpa and Grandma were Catholic back in Sicily, but when they moved to the United States, the only Italian-speaking church in Syracuse was the Italian Christian Assembly Church. Even though I was not yet born, their decision to change from Catholic to Pentecostal Protestants changed my family tree forever.

Grandpa established a truck farm to make provision for his family of seven: Josephine, Samuel, Frank, Frances, John, Emmanuel, and my mom, Marie. Grandpa grew carrots, corn, lettuce, radishes, tomatoes, and more in the black muckland. He sold the vegetables at a local farmer's market. I remember going to the market as a child, riding in the front seat of Grandpa's truck on Grandma's lap. It was an outdoor stand and local farmers came there regularly. Today the outdoor market still exists in Syracuse, but not with all the hustle and bustle of the original Italian families who built it. My cousin's daughter now runs the family store at the market, "Buda's Meat & Produce."

I have memories of my grandpa wearing his glasses as he sat at the kitchen table reading his big Italian Bible. I would climb up on his lap that was mostly full of his tummy and listen as he read. I saw that he had a passion for the Word of God. My grandma never learned to read English, so her Italian Bible was very precious to her as well.

I lived on the farm for the first seven years of my life. I have great memories of those early years with the love of grandparents, aunts, uncles, and cousins all around. We lived with Grandpa and Grandma until Dad built a house next door.

All these memories flooded through my mind as we headed back to the farm that day. I had so much joy when I lived on the family farm. As Al and I drove down the nine-hundred-foot driveway to visit this childhood memory … I was heartbroken. Tears came to my eyes. The once pristine farm was now an overgrown swamp. Our home built by my Dad had burned down a number of years before, and now we couldn't even drive to Grandpa's farmhouse because of trees that had fallen across the driveway. The ruts were so bad that we were forced to stop. The black muckland, which had once been so cared for, was totally hidden by the wild weeds that had taken over. Grandma and Grandpa's house sat abandoned.

All the blood, sweat, and tears that my grandparents had poured into the ground appeared to be gone. Was there an inheritance that had been lost? Was there something to pick up? Years ago my cousin took over the farm, but his vision for the farm was different than Grandpa's. As a businessman, he found it cheaper to buy vegetables rather than growing them himself. As well, my cousin quickly learned that what made the black muckland fertile was that it was a swamp. Every spring came the never-ending challenge of transforming the swamp back into farmland by pumping the water into the dikes. The pumps had to run 24 hours a day to keep up. Eventually the amount of time to reclaim the land each spring was not worth it.

The new formula has worked. My cousin is experiencing far greater financial success. But my heart still hurt.

I was shaken, but I knew the ground had served our family well for many years. Credentials had been earned even though the farm now sat empty. The entrepreneurial spirit that had been on my grandpa had moved to my cousin who ran with it. By standing on Grandpa's shoulders my cousin went higher and farther. But the little farm, along with my childhood memories, were now dimming recollections. Are there some things from the past, even good things, that we have to let go of to move forward in our godly assignment?

Interestingly, my husband Al's grandfather was also an entrepreneur. As a dairy farmer, he was the first to deliver milk to homes around his small town in Pennsylvania. Having lived through the Depression, Grandpa was very conservative with his finances. Upon his death, the money he had saved blessed his four grandchildren with $40,000 each. Every one of us stewarded our money as best  we could. Al's older sister invested much of her inheritance into Kingdom work. Al's brother bought land, Al's younger sister adopted a precious baby girl, and we built our first home. Because of Grandpa's entrepreneurship and sacrifice, we were all blessed financially.

Life took an unexpected twist for us and we needed to sell our newly-built home after just four years. With the closures of several prominent companies, the local housing market had taken a hit. There were over 10,000 single-family homes for sale in our county. After an agonizing fourteen months on the market, our home finally sold. We lost $40,000 on the sale. What happened to our inheritance?

Sometimes God asks us to give Him what we hold tightly in our hand so that He can take us to the next level. We obviously had something to learn about supernatural provision. We needed to know beyond a shadow of doubt where we were called to be and what we were called to do. We had to know that it was God's plan and not ours.

During the fourteen-month delay, we pondered if we had truly heard God about selling the house and moving. We had job opportunities in several other states, but we couldn't accept a job until the house sold. We were excited to move to a new state and have a fresh start in ministry. We asked our friends to pray for our house to sell. We bound the devil from keeping our house from selling. We didn't recognize that God had things to teach us before He would release us.

We attended special meetings led by an out-of-town minister we had never met, Dennis Wiedrick. All I remember is that at the end of the meeting, he called all the pastors to come to the altar. After Dennis prayed, all of us pastors were laying on the floor in the presence of God. We heard Dennis speak over this group, "You are gatekeepers of the city and will be instrumental in seeing your city (Buffalo) come back to life."

As we got in the car, I asked Al if this meant we were staying in Buffalo? (Note: neither of us wanted to!) We struggled with this question for ten days. Finally we both said yes to God. We were willing to stay in Buffalo if that was His will. That week our house sold to a couple that had come to our first open house fourteen months before. Seems rather obvious that we were a bit late in saying Yes to God! What we thought was the devil—not selling our house—was really the Lord keeping us in Buffalo for our next assignment. As Jesus said, "Not my will, but Yours be done" (Luke 22:42).

Following God is always a challenge, but we believe He orders our steps. Oftentimes He is just waiting for the right response from us so that He can release His best to us. About that $40,000 we "lost" in the sale? We know that God has a purpose and a plan. Just like my grandpa's farm, we know God had a purpose. We believe God will continue to provide for our every need. So we trust HIM! We have sown. We will reap.

When my mom was pregnant with me, our family moved from

Stanley, North Dakota, where my dad pastored an Assemblies of God church, to Syracuse, New York, where he took an associate pastor position at the Oswego Assembly of God church. It was a 60-mile drive each Sunday.

Something happened there that I don't begin to understand. My dad, who had attended an Assemblies of God college and pastored Assemblies of God churches, chose to leave his Pentecostal denomination and become the pastor of an evangelical church in North Syracuse.

Given the Pentecostal impact of my great grandfather Awrey, I now look back on this as a season of generational loss. Both my mom and dad had grown up "Pentecostal," but by the time I was born, they had left their roots and moved to a safer and more predictable evangelical denomination. I don't regret this because it gave me a very strong biblical foundation in my upbringing. But now I wonder what was lost and why was it lost?

My Aunt Cassie told me that my Grandpa Buda used to preach and prophesy regularly at his church. My Uncle Manny, her husband, traveled as a powerful singing evangelist and regularly prophesied over people. My Uncle Frank was a Pentecostal pastor. My Aunt Josephine attended Elim Bible Institute, a Pentecostal school, and planned to be a missionary before she married. What happened to these godly Pentecostal mantles? As I look at the generations around me, I recognize how difficult it has been to carry the family spiritual inheritance. You cannot force it on anyone. Only God can draw a person to Himself. Every one of us must choose whether to pursue God or not.

How powerful we would be if the last generation was running at full speed when they passed the baton to the next generation running at full speed! In a relay race, there are four runners. The second, third, and fourth runners are much faster than the first runner because the first runner starts from a dead stop. Oh, if we could only run alongside the generation before us and pick up the mantle, taking it to the next level before we passed it on! (Note: sometimes the mantle needs to be laundered first. Perhaps it has been tainted or dirtied and needs to be cleaned up a bit. It's never a bad idea to cleanse your family tree through the blood of Christ before putting it on.)

I remember the time we accidentally put diesel instead of gasoline in our car. A few miles down the road our car sputtered and died. The bad gas did not destroy the car engine. Cars are designed with a gas filter just for this purpose. Once the gas filter was changed and the diesel drained out, the car ran just fine.

I recommend as you pursue your generational inheritance, you ask God to filter it through the Blood of Jesus. Ask God to cleanse your inheritance. Every negative trait has a positive counterpart. Ask God to help you pick up everything you were meant to carry—nothing more, nothing less.

My prayer for you:

> **Lord, help us to see our "family farm," pick up and clean off what we are meant to carry, and run with gusto our leg of the race. With our hand firmly in Yours, help us to powerfully pass on the mantle that was entrusted to us in a cleaner condition and stronger position to the next generation.**

Chapter 6

Where Do I Start?

Puzzles fascinate me. Usually hundreds of pieces, sometimes thousands of pieces, but it doesn't matter. You settle in knowing that it is going to require lots of time to put it together. Fortunately the picture on the front of the box gives you clues as you choose colors and shapes and patterns. Eventually the fear sets in if you bought the puzzle second hand—what if I'm missing some pieces??

Why do people spend hours putting puzzles together? Do they like a challenge? Is it a relaxing hobby? Are they killing time? Will the final product be worth it?

Recovering your generational inheritance is like assembling a massive, multi-layered puzzle. If you start this grand adventure, recognize that you are signing up for an epic marathon, not just a hundred yard dash. You will go down many dead end streets, examine many leads, ask questions that bring unexpected (good and bad) results, give up and quit, pick a piece up and start again, cry, laugh, rejoice, and repent before you claim your treasures.

Just remember that God wants you to recover your generational inheritance far more than you could ever imagine. He is going with you on the journey to make sure you don't miss a single important piece of your puzzle. When you are congratulating yourself on your key find, He may be in the background asking, "Who do you think steered you there?"

You might ask, "Where do I start?" Hopefully reading this book is a start. But please don't start with my book. Start with spending time with the Father. It is probably God who put it on your heart to do this kind of family research, so first pray and ask Him to order your steps as you pursue your family inheritance. As God leads the process, He will bring supernatural results even as you just crack open the door.

Next you might go to your living relatives, friends, and neighbors who knew your family. On my mother's side, I remember returning to my childhood home on the farm soon after I was married. We went to the Stagnita's home, our old next-door neighbor. Mrs. Stagnita embraced me, calling me "Mary, Mary" (my mother's name) in her rich Italian accent. I looked so much like my mom that Mrs. Stagnita immediately recognized me. Oh the memories that old neighbors are ready to share.

Interview the family and see if any puzzle pieces shake free. You may discover a family member who has already begun to fill out the family tree. On my dad's side, my Aunt Esther put together a family picture storybook and made copies for the whole family. It gives a running history of our family from her perspective. As I read through this storybook, I was encouraged, but I had more questions.

In addition to the storybook, Aunt Esther also wrote a biography of my Grandfather in which she tracked the family dysfunction and abuse in which she grew up. It was hard for me to read. Believe me, not every story you hear is going to be warm and fuzzy. You may want to put on your battle armor.

Perhaps your family has an old family Bible in which is recorded the births, marriages, and deaths of those who went before you. You may have to dig through an attic or two, but sometimes those Bibles are still around just because no one likes to throw away old Bibles. Check for diaries of family members.

Go to the county seat where the family lived to get birth, marriage and death records. Staying on my dad's side, when we returned to Mimosa, Ontario, where the Awrey family resided, the county had an Awrey file that was at least one inch thick. It listed births, deaths, land acquisitions and sales. It even described the land my great-great grandfather Awrey donated to build a community schoolhouse. As education was important to him, decades later great-great grandfather's son, Daniel, would build four schools around the world. Valuing education was part of the generational DNA.

From the Canadian neighbors, I found out that every June, the Awrey family has a family reunion. Al and I decided to attend the next one and discovered how unique we were as U.S. citizens in a mostly Canadian family tree. When we arrived, there were several sign in sheets, one for each Awrey ancestor. Every attendee signed in under his or her forefather. Years ago, each family had 8-10 children so it was very interesting to find which branch of the family tree I was connected to.

Moving back to my mother's Italian side of the family, it's fun to hang out with Italians! As Olive Garden reminds us, "We're All Family Here!" Italians value relationships. It's our tradition to attend the annual Italian festival in Buffalo, NY. We walked into a tent that specialized in genealogical research on Italian families who came through Ellis Island. Keep your eyes open. You never know where you'll find help on your search.

Of course, the web can be a rich source for research. My dad's name was Sam Smith, so a web search would turn up too much unrelated information to be useful. On the other hand, my dad's mom was an Awrey, a unique name easily researched on the web. When Al was doing a research paper on Daniel Awrey for the Society for Pentecostal Studies in Lakeland, FL, he lost a lot of sleep as one web link would take him to the next and the next and the next. Al felt a bit like an ancient explorer discovering new worlds. Al accessed research libraries not only in the U.S., but also in the Netherlands, Germany, Great Britain, Hong Kong, and around the world.

You can't miss the ads for Ancestry.com®). Their website declares, "See what makes your family story truly one of a kind. From beloved traditions and special places to quirky characters and wild stories—let Ancestry help you discover all the pieces that make your family story like no other." This and other web resources may be worth investigating.

Nowadays, I talk to many people who have gotten their DNA tested to discover their roots. They buy a kit, swab their mouth, send it in, and receive a printed report with suggestions of country or region of origin. I haven't done this yet, but I expect I will. Some have discovered unknown brothers and sisters. Others have uncovered family secrets that had been buried for generations. Even murders have been solved through DNA research.

Don't be afraid of what you might find. Dirt in the family tree does not disqualify you from the plan of God for your life. Just read the Bible. In some generations, people turned away from God, but often their children turned back to God. No matter what those before you chose, you can choose for you and your house to follow the Lord. Whatever you uncover, God knew all this since before you were born. Cover generational sin with the blood of Jesus. Ask God to cleanse you from guilt and shame from the past. Embrace who God made you to be.

If no one has started a family tree, volunteer to start the research. If you are like us, we wish we had started the process when key family members were still alive. Unfortunately, we didn't get serious about the process until we were in our 50's. The younger you start the easier and more complete the process will be. And someday other relatives will bless you when their curiosity builds and they are ready to know more about their family history.

Initiate a family reunion. That is what I did with the Buda family in 2019. No had brought the family together since Grandma Buda died in the early 1960's. I was shocked at the response—26 family members from 5 states and 8 cities. That weekend I saw relatives that I hadn't seen in over 40 years. I was excited to reconnect. What drew them? Was it the sweet memories of childhood? Why had so many chosen to come? What does it say about

the bond of being part of a family?

Grandpa and Grandma came from Sicily as a young married couple. They had seven children. Each of them married and eventually scattered throughout the country, with a few staying around Syracuse. I was focused on getting together the first cousins. When I called,

they answered. Even those who were unable to come responded.

Family relationships are strange. We don't all live in the same area. We don't like the same food or have the same hobbies. We don't even all follow the same God. But there is a glue. Do people like to remember the past? What was everyone else expecting as they came? Did some even wonder why they agreed to come? Are we all getting older and wondering how long we will still walk this earth? Are we seeking roots?

So why did 26 people come to the Buda reunion? And why did I call it? What was God's agenda for the day?

- We returned to the family farm for a visit, but of course it was completely overgrown. What did the family think as we crawled through swamp grass that was over our heads?
- We returned to the market where Grandpa sold his vegetables, but it has changed so much. It is more of a flea market than a farmer's market.

All of us started reminiscing, calling up long forgotten childhood memories. I recalled sitting in Grandpa's stall, watching so many people buying what he sold at the market. But every family member took pictures of the key current reminder of our family's legacy—the big sign reading "Buda's Meat & Produce" that welcomes every shopper to the Regional Market in Syracuse. The family name lives on.

Even though we hadn't seen each other in years or even decades, there was an immediate trust among the family members. Maybe the old roots still have life. We had a wonderful time laughing and remembering. My prayer is that God would awaken something inside each of my family members that will stir a new and deeper passion for God.

"Tell your children about it in the years to come, and let your children tell their children. Pass the story down from generation to generation" (Joel 1:3 NLT).

"But watch out! Be careful never to forget what you yourself have seen. Do not let these memories escape from your mind as long as you live! And be sure to pass them on to your children and grandchildren" (Deuteronomy 4:9 NLT).

The Bible is full of stories. Like your family, there are high highs and low lows. There are victories and defeats. There is death and life, blessing and curse, survival and endurance.

The Bible is a generational history book. As a history book, the Bible recounts the stories of its heroes, warts and all. In fact it may include more than we might if we were writing the family history. Would we include Noah's drunkenness and nakedness? Would we include David's adulterous relationship with Beersheba? Would we include Peter's denial?

If you were choosing, you might lean toward the hero rather than the villain role. But family trees often have an assortment of both. Don't be afraid to look at both. Let the generations that follow learn not only from our successes, but also our failures. Be honest, but not hurtful.

Look for Christians in your family tree. You might even find a pastor or two. A friend showed me pictures that were given to him of the church his great-grandfather pastored in Buffalo. Although the church building is gone, my friend has pictures to prove a key family member was a God follower.

Appreciate the journey as you document your family history to be preserved for generations to come. There are great joys in finding traits in yourself that came down through previous generations. So pick up a shovel and start digging for godly gold.

Chapter 7

A Jubilee Year of Recovery

WOW! TURNING 50 WAS A BIG DEAL! Social stigma regularly reminded me that I was just getting old and heading toward antique status. But God sees aging differently.

When I was 49, we were sitting with Pastor Ron Burgio in his office.

He mentioned that he was scheduled to speak at the Assembly of God Church in Oswego, NY. Much to his surprise, I got excited and asked if we could go with him. It turns out this was the last Assembly of God Church in which my dad worked. He served as the associate pastor. I was dedicated in that church as a baby. At the end of dad's service there, he chose to leave the Assemblies to become an evangelical pastor in a denomination in which he served for 50 years.

Pastor Ron said we were welcome to join him and gave us the dates he would be ministering, July 9-12, 2006. I asked if I could bless the congregation and stand in the gap for my dad. I didn't know exactly how or why my father had left that church. Something in me said it had not been on the best of terms. I wondered if he had chosen to lay down a mantle in regard to the supernatural. Did he lay down part of my heritage as well? Had he been hurt there? I pondered.

As we looked at the days, Sunday through Wednesday, we decided to drive the three hours and attend the Monday, July 10th evening service.

At the service, Pastor Ron invited me to speak to the congregation. God gave me grace to honor my dad in this place that he had walked away from for reasons I did not know. I publicly stood in the gap for my dad, asking forgiveness of the church for any way he may have responded badly. I prayed a blessing over them. No one present remembered my dad, but that didn't matter. Sometimes we need to stand in the gap and ask forgiveness for what has happened in the past in order for God to release a blessing on them and us.

> "I looked for someone who might rebuild the wall of righteousness that guards the land. I searched for someone to stand in the gap in the wall so I wouldn't have to destroy the land, but I found no one" (Ezekiel 22:30 NLT).

That night at the service, July 10th, Al felt led to write two checks for $50 each. One was to the church from our Set Free account and the other was to the pastor from our personal account. I agreed, sensing he was hearing from God. Although we didn't fully understand all that we had done, we felt that we had obeyed God and completed an assignment.

In the middle of that same night, I got up for my devotions. Out of curiosity I began to research "Jubilee" with my 50th in view. The following Scripture popped out. Remember we were at the service **July 10th**:

> "Count off seven sabbaths years—seven times seven years—so that the seven sabbaths years amount to a **period of forty-nine years**. Then have the trumpet sounded everywhere on the **tenth**

day of the seventh month; on the Day of Atonement sound the trumpet throughout your land. Consecrate the fiftieth year and proclaim liberty throughout the land to all its inhabitants. It shall be a jubilee for you; each one of you is **to return to his family property** and each to his own clan. The fiftieth year shall be a jubilee for you; do not sow and do not reap what grows of itself or harvest the untended vines. For it is a jubilee and is to be holy for you; eat only what is taken directly from the fields. In this Year of Jubilee everyone is to return to his own property.

"If you sell land to any of your own people or buy land from them, do not take advantage of each other. **You are to buy from your own people on the basis of the number of years since the Jubilee.** And they are to sell to you on the basis of the number of years left for harvesting crops" (Leviticus 25:8-15 NIV).

Amazing—only once in my lifetime would I be 49 years old on the **tenth day of the seventh month**—July 10th. (Ok, I know some of you Jewish scholars are saying the Hebrew calendar and the Western calendar have different months with different numbers of days, but for me this was way too cool to be a coincidence!) Remember, when Pastor Ron told us he was speaking in Oswego, he gave us the option of coming one of four nights. Was God playing with us, ordering our steps so that we chose to come on that specific Monday night? Regardless, I was at the Oswego church picking up my family mantle on the perfect day! Wow!

Unknown to us, the two checks we wrote were buying back "family inheritance" (verse 15). We decided on the price as we wrote the checks. I still don't fully understand what it all meant, but I know that God's blessing was definitely focused on my Jubilee Year.

Al and I prayed, filtering this experience through the blood of Jesus. I chose to pick up and clean off any spiritual inheritance that I was meant to have. I sensed God allowing me to pick up a lost mantle. Within days a new download of spiritual wisdom and authority manifested itself.

Within three months of that church service, I found out for the first time about my great-grandfather, Daniel Awrey. What might happen to you as you climb into the seemingly dark cave to explore what has been lost in your family inheritance? I prophesy that the dead, dry, disconnected bones of your past will come to life!

I know I'm not there yet, but I stand amazed at how God is continuing to work in me. In my Jubilee year, He returned to me what had been stolen in my infancy. Like me, some of you are feeling the intensity of the battle for your inheritance. Like David, when you pursue, may you recover all that the Father has for you.

Anticipate growing older, especially your Jubilee year. You earned every one of those gray hairs. God has some abundant blessings in store for you. Don't let the enemy steal one day that your Father has prepared for you. The world says you are getting old ... over the hill ... out to pasture ... useless. God says you are blessed ... mature ... an overcomer ... a seasoned warrior! As you have sown, so may you reap bountifully! You have earned credentials in the heavenlies that are unseen to you. Now is the time to recover all the enemy has tried to steal. This season will be your most rewarding time yet. More doors will open than you ever imagined. Keep knocking. Supernatural surprises ahead!

Chapter 8

Putting the Puzzle Together

IF YOU ARE LIKE ME, YOU EMPTY the puzzle box, spreading all the pieces on the table. Then you sort the pieces, separating the edge pieces from the middle pieces. Next you may sort by color or pattern. But what if you can match only a couple of pieces at a time? What if you recognize something that only partly resembles a color you saw before? What if you don't realize a piece got stuck in the box or fell to the floor or got hidden by your brother? The good news is that you can refer back to the picture on the box to know what the finished puzzle will look like.

If only recovering a generational inheritance was that easy. I have learned there is no picture on a box to know what my inheritance will look like when I recover all. Even after working on my generational puzzle for more than thirteen years, I'm still not sure what pieces I'm missing. I'm not sure if I'm 20% done or 80% done. I'm not even sure how much of the puzzle is not mine to finish but rather for my children and grandchildren to continue.

Al was at a leaders meeting in Texas when he met a pastor from Liberia, West Africa, Apostle Judah Vah. After a brief conversation, Apostle Vah invited us to come and speak at the sixth year anniversary conference at his church near Monrovia, Liberia. The conference theme was "Advancing

Kingdom Works beyond Limits."
Twelve pastors/congregations were
coming together for the conference.

We had talked about going to
Africa, ministering on our fifth continent, returning to the place Awrey
had died. But suddenly the talk
became real. Should we accept? We
knew Liberia was just coming out
of the Ebola pandemic. After prayer
and pondering, we decided to accept Judah Vah's invitation. This puzzle piece had the color of Liberia, the nation where my great-grandfather
preached and then died and was buried in 1913 at age 43. We wondered
how this puzzle piece might fit.

Knowing that my great-grandfather had died in Liberia, I was quite
concerned about our health and safety. Thankfully, in the days leading
up to our trip, God brought us to Word of Life Ministries, a church in
Niagara Falls pastored by our friend Bishop Jesse Scott. After we finished
preaching there, Bishop Scott brought his elders and intercessors forward
to lay hands on us. This predominantly black congregation laid hands on
us for our assignment in Africa. They sensed my concerns and prayed for
me powerfully. The Lord spoke to me during that prayer, "You shall live
and not die!" After the prayer, a burden lifted and we felt well covered as
we headed into unknown territories. Time to recover another puzzle piece.

Note: Sometimes when you are picking up a generational inheritance,
you need to let others help bear the burdens with you. Christianity is a
team sport. Lean into your team's strengths.

We went to Africa blissfully ignorant of what we would find there.
Liberia experienced civil war from 1989 through 2003. With a population
of five million, one million people died during the civil wars. A decade

later, the Ebola outbreak occurred which closed down the only international-al airport for one year. Imagine no businessperson able to come to or leave Liberia for a year. Some churches shut down all public services for fear of spreading the disease. The infrastructure and economy were destroyed.

Today, most of the country is run on generators. There is a total lack of healthy tap water. With so many tragic deaths, there are orphanages, Christian schools, and medical centers everywhere. The vast majority of these are run by churches, mission boards, and non-profits who have stepped up to help. Most of the money to run them comes from the West. Liberia is a country with overwhelming need.

We knew little of this when we arrived. However, we did know we had an assignment from God. At the conference, we preached and ministered fifteen times in twelve days to pastors and leaders from twelve churches, but we knew that this was not the only reason we had come.

With the favor of God combined with our friendship with Bishop  Stephan Booze of Niagara Falls, we were introduced to the Chaplain General of Liberia, Bishop John Paul Chea. Bishop Chea has a double mantle. On the one hand he runs an orphanage for 85 children. On the other hand, as Chaplain General of the nation, he is a trusted minister and counselor to the most powerful political leaders of Liberia. Bishop Chea opened the door for us to minister one-on-one with the Speaker of the House of Representatives. Surprisingly, the Speaker asked me if I was afraid to return to Liberia because my great-grandfather died there. I was able to give testimony to him of the word from the Lord, "I would live and not die."

Before we left for Liberia, I made a passing comment to Al, "Wouldn't it be wonderful if we met someone who had somehow been impacted by Daniel Awrey. Of course, this seemed unimaginable. Over one hundred years had gone by since Awrey's death. He had less than two months of ministry in Liberia before his death. This seemed impossible. But God!

We don't have much that belonged to Daniel Awrey, but we do have a copy of the last letter he wrote before his death. This letter traces the names of the towns where he ministered during those last weeks of his life. The clues suggest he was buried somewhere in Maryland County in the rural part of Liberia. To help pinpoint his grave, Bishop Chea set up a meet-

ing with the representative of Mary-land County, Representative Bhofal Chambers. As we spoke to Repre-sentative Chambers about Daniel Awrey's visit in 1913, he said, "1913 is important to my family as well." We were shocked and fully attentive for the rest of the story.

Chambers shared his family story from 1913. He showed us a picture of his great-great-grand-father, William Wade Harris, who was an advocate for the poor. The gov-ernment so hated Harris that they imprisoned him for 3 years from 1910 to 1913. While in prison, Harris had a spiritual experience with an angelic visitation. He left his denominational church and became Pentecostal. After his release, Harris started the first indigenous Pentecostal denomination in Africa. Representative Chambers told us people called his great-great-grand-father Harris a prophet (The same is true for Daniel Awrey). Harris not only impacted Liberia, but also went on to the Ivory Coast and Ghana. The denomination that he founded totaled over 1 million members.

Something jumped inside me. Could this be a key puzzle piece I came to Liberia to find? As soon as I returned to my hotel, I googled Daniel Awrey and William Wade Harris—**I found them in the same paragraph** in the book *Azusa Street* written by Cecil Robeck. Wow! It was a supernatural surprise that God allowed us to connect with a leader whose family tree was impacted by Daniel Awrey more than 100 years before! God is mind-blowing!

Here is the excerpt from Cecil Robeck's book, *Azusa Street Mission & Revival*:

> In September 1913 the Azusa Street missionary evangelist Daniel Awrey left his young family in Los Angeles while he traveled to Liberia. He wrote back that on the night of October 9, 1913 he had preached "to a large congregation in the Apostolic Faith Church" in Monrovia—mostly likely McCauley's mission. The next day Awrey continued his travels. Unfortunately, he soon contracted a case of malaria and died on December 2, 1913, before he could complete his trip.
>
> Sadly, the foundational work of Mrs. Hutchins, Lucy Farrow, and the Batman family, the Cooks, Lee, McKinney and the McCauleys have disappeared completely from all official histories of missions in Liberia. McCauley's mission was the first permanent Pentecostal congregation on the continent of Africa, and it may ultimately prove to be the source of the Pentecostal theology and experience that produced Prophet William Wade Harris and his millions-strong Harrist Church of the Ivory Coast (Cote d'Ivoire). It was African Americans, not whites, who established his congregation. Their missionary activities push the documented beginnings of Pentecostal members in Liberia back two full years from the date reported in every Pentecostal mission history of Liberia today.

In each of these cases, the missionaries to Liberia were African-American; their stories open a chapter on African Americans' role in the early worldwide spread of the Pentecostal message. These missionaries raised to new heights the vision for missions within the Pentecostal tradition, at the same time modeling a trust in God to meet all their needs as they sought to fulfill the Great Commission.

But there was still an unexpected blessing to come. Our friends who hosted the conference at which we were the keynote speakers, Judah and Marian Vah, chose to rename their brand new school, Daniel Awrey King Kids Academy. What an honor.  A century after his death Daniel Awrey is once again touching Liberia. Although Daniel Awrey died before completing his planned mission in Liberia, he lives on through the lives of students in Liberia.

The school in Liberia seems an especially fitting tribute for Daniel Awrey. He believed in education. During his ministry career, he started four schools around the world, including ones in Ohio, Oklahoma, Canton, China and Shanghai, China. I can only imagine how proud he would be to touch children who may someday lead Liberia into its God-given destiny.

Daniel Awrey's legacy lives on. Because I faced my fear and went to Liberia, I hold in my hand another puzzle piece. I'm not yet sure where it fits, but it is intriguing.

One more note of interest. In December, 2017, Liberia held national elections. Our friend, Representative Bhofal Chambers, was elected the Speaker of the House. Another leader we prayed for while there is now the President of Liberia, President Weah. Is God starting to work on another part of my puzzle? Will we ever return to Liberia? Do we hold any keys that could advocate for the poor in this needy country? Only God knows, but He does order our steps.

What about you? Like a detective, some of the leads you follow will be wild goose chases. Other leads are more costly or painful than you expect. If God hid a significant puzzle piece in a place you didn't want to go or with a person you didn't want to connect with, how desperate are you to recover all the enemy has stolen? Pray before the journey, pray on the journey, invite others to pray with you. Remember, it is okay to allow others to help carry you with their prayers. Putting puzzles together is always easier, faster, and more fun with friends!

Chapter 9

Our Visit to Sicily

In late 2017, we were invited to go to Israel. It was remarkable to walk through the Bible, stepping onto soil where the Bible stories which I read as a child actually happened. I imagined I was walking on the same roads  where Samuel's mother came to the temple, where Jesus fed the 5000, the Garden where Jesus wept great drops of blood, and the one place that differentiates Christianity from every other religion—the **Empty Tomb**. My heart leapt as we stood in the Upper Room, the place where some believe both the Last Supper as well as the Day of Pentecost took place.

In the Upper Room, my mind raced back to my great-grandfather, Daniel Awrey, who spent time in the Holy Land more than 100 years ago. He probably visited this same room. Like us, Awrey probably prayed here. My heart overflowed with joy at the mystical connection with a lover of God from my own family tree.

In late 2019, we cele-brated our first trip to Sicily, the homeland of my moth-er's parents. We visited their hometown, Linguaglossa. The town sits at the base of Mount Etna, an active vol-cano. Interestingly, I felt a similar joy to my time in

Israel. In Israel, I followed the footsteps of Jesus. In Sicily, I followed the footsteps of my grandparents, Anthony and Rose Buda. At 15 years of age, my grandmother married my grandfather. They were first cousins so they shared the same last name—Buda. When Grandma was 16 years old, she and Grandpa immigrated to America.

Linguaglossa is old (founded 1566), and the buildings are covered with black volcanic ash from centuries of the daily "sniffles" from Mount Etna. The churches are old, with the current Parish Church being constructed in 1613. I immediately recognized that my grandparents daily walked on these same streets and looked at these same old churches. I don't know which church they belonged to, but I know they were lovers of God so they certainly attended one of them.

We headed to City Hall to track my relatives. (Note: when researching, it is important to have exact names (not nicknames) of family members, dates of birth and death, etc.) Some records were on microfiche, others in files which required time and effort to locate. As you might imagine, records more than 100 years old are not at anyone's fingertips. It was much more involved than I made time for. Ah well, next time....

The town clerk was able to tell us that there was a local business owned by a Buda. The business sold gardening supplies. Away we went on an unplanned adventure. What a joy it was to talk to another "Buda." With limited time and language challenges, we couldn't dig deep enough to be absolutely certain that this Buda is of the same bloodlines as my grandparents, but it is a small town (population 5,300) so we assume she was. As we hugged goodbye, my heart jumped inside, believing that God had once again come through on our behalf to fulfill the desires of my heart. A prepared path, divine connections, and supernatural surprises!

Our last stop in Linguaglossa was the most important—FOOD! As a Sicilian, I've had antipasto for years. But the <u>hot antipasto</u> at this hole-in-the-wall restaurant was the best ever—as beautiful as it was flavorful. That memory will stick with me forever.

For me, family names that I had never seen back home were everywhere in Sicily. While walking through another Sicilian town, Taormina, my eyes were drawn to a store selling purses, shoes, and other accessories. The name of the store was—**MUSUMECI**. My mother's sister Josephine's married name was Musumeci. I took a picture and immediately texted it to my cousins back home.

After returning home to Buffalo, we learned that in Europe, churches are primary keepers of the family historical records. (Note: when you are researching family history, remember that churches usually keep detailed records of births, deaths, baptisms, and more.) If we were to return to Sicily again, we would make an appointment to explore the church records.

As we flew back home, I took time to ponder my grandparents' journey to the U.S. My flight home was tough—eleven hours cramped in economy class. I don't think my grandparents would pity me as they took weeks for the same journey by ship.

I would like to go to the Immigration Museum at Ellis Island, their point of arrival. But if you had relatives who came through Ellis Island, go to https://www.libertyellisfoundation.org/passenger to find their date of arrival, age, ship name, and so much more at your fingertips. (Ancestry. com, FamilySearch.org, and other sites on the internet, as well as courthouses, libraries, and archives are also good places to locate records. There is always more research to do on your family tree.)

As my grandparents considered immigrating to America, what were their dreams? Why did they choose to leave their home country to start a life together in a whole new world? Did they know the cost of leaving their culture, language, and many family members behind? If they were still alive, I would love to hear their stories, step into their dreams, and ask question after question about their journey.

I am reminded of the story of Joshua when he led the Israelites across the Jordan River:

> When all the people had crossed the Jordan, the Lord said to Joshua, "Now choose twelve men, one from each tribe. Tell them, 'Take twelve stones from the very place where the priests are standing in the middle of the Jordan. Carry them out and pile them up at the place where you will camp tonight.'"
>
> So Joshua called together the twelve men he had chosen—one from each of the tribes of Israel. He told them, "Go into the middle of the Jordan, in front of the Ark of the Lord your God. Each of you must pick up one stone and carry it out on your

shoulder—twelve stones in all, one for each of the twelve tribes of Israel. We will use these stones to build a memorial. **In the future your children will ask you, 'What do these stones mean?' Then you can tell them, 'They remind us that the Jordan River stopped flowing when the Ark of the Lord's Covenant went across.'** These stones will stand as a memorial among the people of Israel forever" (Joshua 4:1-7 NLT).

What questions did the children ask about the stones in Joshua's day? How did the older generation respond? Can you imagine hearing the stories told firsthand by eyewitnesses testifying to the miracles that brought them to their family farm in Israel? Think of the wide-eyed children who heard true stories of slavery, plagues, walls of water, giants, and more!?! The stones proclaimed life-giving, faith-building, obstacle-overcoming stories.

What *"stones"* have you set up to help your children and grandchildren remember their spiritual and physical heritage? One of the *"stones"* my mother-in-law left behind is a simple children's book that tells the Christmas story. It is old and tattered from decades of family use. Each Christmas, the older generation of Warners has gathered the family and read through this precious book. When my sons were young, we read it as a family. As I wrote about this *"stone,"* I decided I would read it to my grandchildren next Christmas.

Do not wait to gather *memorial stones* for your children and grandchildren. Do it now! Ask God to show you *stones, stories, and testimonies* today. Build on the godly parts of previous generations. Make memories together. Share with your children the life-giving stories of your past, alongside the life-giving stories farther back in your family tree. Don't let testimonies be lost, but rather let them be passed down as a family treasure.

God has given you a legacy that needs to be remembered. May the generational credentials that you have earned be the starting blocks from which the next generation can get a running start to race faster, jump higher, run farther than we could have imagined!

> "They triumphed over him by the blood of the Lamb and by the word of their **testimony**...." (Revelation 12:11a NIV).

Chapter 10

Th∈R∈ is Pow∈R in the Clos∈t

"But when you pray, go away by yourself, shut the door behind you, and pray to your Father in private. Then your Father, who sees everything, will reward you" (Matthew 6:6 NLT).

Growing up in the Smith family, our weekday morning routine was to eat as a family at the breakfast table, finishing with family devotions. My Dad read a portion of Scripture, then a daily devotional, and concluded by going around the table expecting each of us to pray. Finally, we recited the Lord's Prayer together. This created an opportunity to pray for one another, to remember the importance of the Bible, and to agree that prayer works. I don't remember anything profound from family devotions, but it was a discipline that developed a rhythm for my own consistent devotions as I grew older.

Years later when I was raising my sons, we had nightly devotions before they went to bed. We read a devotional that fit their age, talked about it, and prayed. Today I wish that I had taught them how to pray better. It became more of a discipline and less of a "heart time" with God.

I was very intrigued when I found an article written by my Great-grandfather Awrey about his family. When he wrote the article in 1910, he was living in Hong Kong with his family. He penned his memories of family devotions…. "My parents had family prayer as long as I can remember; my mother would sing and rejoice, which I could not then understand."

I had never been in another home of a family that had family devotions. I thought we were unique. Little did I know that this tradition had been passed down from generation to generation for at least five generations. Will my children continue the chain? Have I taught them enough about prayer, Bible study, and intimacy with God that they will make time to do it and then be intentional to pass it on?

In 2010, we were invited to return to Hong Kong. You may remember that when we moved to Hong Kong in the 1980s, we had no idea that generations before me had lived there. I shared that revelation in Chapter 1.

Let me remind you that in Hong Kong I had an unexpected pregnancy. I was pregnant in a foreign country and culture far from family. To top it all off, after Nathan was born I developed medical complications that required emergency surgery and eventually brought us back to the States. We never returned to Hong Kong.

Fast forward to 2010, twenty-two years later. We are returning to Hong Kong, the place where doctors say I could have died. To say the least, I was less than excited to go.

Before we left for Hong Kong, our friend Stephen Jenks from Eagles

Wings Ministries prophesied, "Beauty for ashes. What was death will be life.... Cinder-**ella** will become Ember-**ella**.... He is rekindling an ember that is now going to be a fire-starting device to restart a fire that was your inheritance in days past... that which is the fire of God that you've been meant to carry into this land will not be extinguished. In Jesus name." As only God can do, Stephen did not have a clue that my great-grandma's name was **Ella**. His words have become even more real as that visit continued to spread a fire in me to uncover my generational inheritance.

Amazingly, when we went to Hong Kong, we left Buffalo on Good Friday (commemorating Jesus' death), flying all day Friday and Saturday as we gained 13 hours. Our first awakening in Hong Kong was Easter Sunday morning (NEW LIFE conquering death!).

A friend, Dr. Larry Keefauver, gave us this word: "The blessing of your great-grandfather's legacy now passes to you. The spiritual wealth and natural blessings of your family's legacy is now your birthright and possession as a godly offspring. On Resurrection Sunday, as you arise in China, so your inheritance will be resurrected through the grace and power of your Lord Jesus Christ. Rejoice. Glorify His Name. Receive all the generational blessings and inheritance laid up for you."

> "The Lord says, 'Good people leave an inheritance to their grandchildren, but the sinner's wealth passes to the godly'" (Proverbs 13:22 NLT).

Make a list of some of the traditions in your family that your parents intentionally included to carry on a godly inheritance. At Christmas time, do you read the Christmas story in the Bible out loud to the family? I mentioned this to one of my friends and she said she wouldn't even know where to find it in the Bible. I bought her a Bible and put a bookmark in the spot so she could find the Christmas story. This simple act changed their family forever.

Teach your children to pray, to hear God's voice personally. If I could do it again, I would do it more intentionally.

My Grandma Smith (Daniel Awrey's daughter) visited while we lived in Missouri after we returned from Hong Kong. She encouraged my son to memorize Scripture. Caleb, at 5 years of age, memorized Psalm 23 because of her influence. After that, whenever we ministered in a church, Caleb would stand on the platform and quote this Psalm. Even though he doesn't remember it today, I believe it must be deep in his spirit. Make the changes now to keep your inheritance alive!

Jesus encouraged his followers, "When thou prayest, enter into thy closet, and when thou hast shut thy door, pray to thy Father.... (Matthew 6:6). I remember my Dad sharing that when he was young, his Mom would go into an actual closet and not want to be disturbed while she spent time with her Father.

Sharon Glasgow, a motivational speaker, tells about Susanna Wesley: "She was married to a preacher. They had 19 children. All except ten died in infancy of which, two grew up to bring millions of souls to Christ. That would be John and Charles Wesley. She struggled to find a secret place to get away with Him. So she advised her children that when they saw her with her apron over her head, that meant she was in prayer and couldn't be disturbed. She was devoted to her walk with Christ, praying for her children and knowledge in the Word no matter how hard life was."

Many of you may have seen the movie, "War Room" (2015), a movie about a seemingly perfect family. Priscilla Shirer portrays the wife who is taught by "Miss Clara," an older, wiser woman. The wife learns principles that she uses in her "prayer closet" to rescue her marriage and family.

So why is there power in the closet? When one learns to daily close the door, study His words, listen to a loving Father's voice, and sense His presence, your life is changed forever. There is faith and hope imparted to you to walk through any test that is before you.

My prayer for the generations that follow me is that they will have passion for God. As I researched the story of my Great-grandfather Awrey, one thing that stood out is he always wanted more of God. He waited on God to meet him wherever he was in the world. He created an atmosphere around him so that others could receive more of God. He loved people so much that he wanted to pass on what he had experienced in his own spiritual walk. He walked out 1 Thessalonians 2:8 (NLT): "We loved you so much that we shared with you not only God's Good News but our own lives, too."

As you read about Daniel in the Bible, he spent much time in the closet. He had a window in his closet so others noticed him praying. Those who noticed were jealous and convinced the king to make a law to stop Daniel from praying to his God.

See Daniel 6:7-11 (NLT):

"We are all in agreement—we administrators, officials, high officers, advisers, and governors—that the king should make a law that will be strictly enforced. Give orders that for the next thirty days any person who prays to anyone, divine or human—except to you, Your Majesty—will be thrown into the den of lions. And now, Your Majesty, issue and sign this law so it cannot be changed, an official law of the Medes and Persians that cannot be revoked." So King Darius signed the law.

"But when Daniel learned that the law had been signed, he went home and knelt down as usual in his upstairs room, with its windows open toward Jerusalem. He prayed three times a day, just as he had always done, giving thanks to his

God. Then the officials went together to Daniel's house and found him praying and asking for God's help."

Daniel was thrown into a lion's den for obeying God rather than man. But Daniel proved that spending time in the closet can turn lions into pussycats. God converted the lion's den from a place of death to a place of authority and of rest. Daniel lived to prove that **spending time with God can shut up lions and still the voices of your critics.**

Daniel 6:16-24 (NLT):

"So at last the king gave orders for Daniel to be arrested and thrown into the den of lions. The king said to him, 'May your God, whom you serve so faithfully, rescue you.'

"A stone was brought and placed over the mouth of the den. The king sealed the stone with his own royal seal and the seals of his nobles, so that no one could rescue Daniel. Then the king returned to his palace and spent the night fasting. He refused his usual entertainment and couldn't sleep at all that night.

"Very early the next morning, the king got up and hurried out to the lions' den. When he got there, he called out in anguish, 'Daniel, servant of the living God! Was your God, whom you serve so faithfully, able to rescue you from the lions?'

"Daniel answered, 'Long live the king! My God sent his angel to shut the lions' mouths so that they would not hurt me, for I have been found innocent in his sight. And I have not wronged you, Your Majesty.'

"The king was overjoyed and ordered that Daniel be lifted from the den. Not a scratch was found on him, for he had trusted in his God.

"Then the king gave orders to arrest the men who had maliciously accused Daniel. He had them thrown into the lions' den, along with their wives and children. The lions leaped on them and tore them apart before they even hit the floor of the den."

Daniel is an example to us that as we spend time in the closet, God will fight our battles for us. He will give us wisdom to walk through any storm that brews around us. He will prepare us ahead of time for whatever our day holds.

I believe there is power in my closet when I spend time with the Father. Prayer: "Lord Jesus, create a never-ending hunger for You first in me, and then in the generations that follow me. Help them to discover the secret power found in the closet and to use it wisely."

Chapter 11

Generational Blessings

HAVE YOU NOTICED HOW OFTEN GENERATIONAL GIFTS and talents repeat themselves? You know ...

- Pastors. A son or daughter grew up in the church and chose to follow in their parents' footsteps.
- Doctors. One of Al's surgeons was a third generation doctor.

The same can be true for politicians, schoolteachers, lawyers, mechanics, etc. In today's world, you can do almost anything you want to do. So why might occupations continue into the third and fourth generations? Could there be an inheritance, a talent, or gifting that comes through the family tree making it easier to develop?

> "... I lay the sins of the parents upon their children; the entire family is affected—even children in the third and fourth generations of those who reject m. **But I lavish unfailing love for a thousand generations on those who love me and obey my commands**" (Exodus 20:5-6 NLT).

I repeat this verse on purpose throughout my book. It is vital to my topic. I am fascinated that as we love, honor, and obey God, He promises to *lavish His unfailing love* on us. I live in the shadow of Niagara Falls. I picture God's love continually pouring down on me like the water of Niagara Falls. Will you step into the Falls with me?

I believe that we should honor those who have gone before us if we are to stand taller and reach higher. To honor someone is *to give high respect, esteem or recognition to him or her.* The Bible repeats nine times the command to honor your father and mother. It is one of the Ten Commandments. It appears in both the New and Old Testament so it would seem that God is trying to get our attention.

> "Honor your father and mother, as the Lord your God command-
> ed you. Then you will live a long, full life in the land the Lord
> your God is giving you" (Deuteronomy 5:16 NLT).

I want to honor the generations who have gone before me. I want to encourage you to uncover and gather the spiritual inheritance you were meant to carry. Search your family history. Be prepared for the good and the bad, but do it anyway. God is not ashamed of your family tree. After all, it got you here. Ask God to cleanse with the Blood of Jesus those pieces that need to be purified and to bring to life those gifts that have been hidden. What if there are inheritances that have already been bought and paid for by generations past that are sitting unclaimed?

I wish that I had written this book when my parents were still alive. I am filled with questions that will go unanswered because family members are already gone. Some of the things that I have uncovered are too disturbing for me to include in my book. If only I could get my older relatives' insights and perspectives, but most of them are gone.

A sermon contrasting honor and dishonor moved me. The main point was that when we dishonor, we teach others to dishonor. God gave the speaker a way to share in an honoring way how God had healed him from the dysfunctional home in which he grew up in. But the speaker didn't focus on his dysfunctional home or attack his parents for the dysfunction. Rather he focused on the journey of healing through which God had brought him. The speaker was obviously healed from dark memories. We all need to choose to guard our mouths as we talk about our family.

> "'Honor your father and mother.' This is the first commandment with a promise: If you honor your father and mother, 'things will go well for you, and you will have a long life on the earth'" Ephesians 6:2-3 (NLT).

Have you pondered that from before you were even conceived God's hand has been all over you? With divine purpose, the Lord ordered the day of your birth, the place of your birth, your birth family, your birth order. You will never know how different a person you would be today if you had been born into a different family. This same principle can still apply even if you are adopted. God still has had a hand in your life. He has never left you or forsaken you.

The Psalmist reminds us in Psalm 139:15-16 (NLT): "You watched me as I was being formed in utter seclusion, as I was woven together in the dark of the womb. You saw me before I was born. Every day of my life was recorded in your book. Every moment was laid out before a single day had passed."

James Goll, a well-known author, suggests seven areas of blessings we can each tap into: biblical promises; family genealogy; ethnic background; church experiences; geographic region (city, state, nation); the meaning of your name; and personal prophetic words. These are life-giving springs of blessing to explore.

1. There Are Promises for You in the Bible

As you study God's Word, it is full of promises that should grab your attention. What does God say about you in His Word? I read that there are 640 blessings of God recorded in the Bible. These are life-changing promises available to us as believers. I sometimes walk to my mirror, look at myself, and read out loud these promises. Acknowledging that God is your Father, repeat the following blessings to help you walk into the full inheritance of God. These are just a few of those blessings to accept and cling to.

"The Lord himself will fight for you. Just stay calm" (Exodus 14:14 NLT).

"Do not be afraid or discouraged, for the Lord will personally go ahead of you. He will be with you; he will neither fail you nor abandon you" (Deuteronomy 31:8 NLT).

"Even when I walk through the darkest valley, I will not be afraid, for you are close beside me. Your rod and your staff protect and comfort me" (Psalm 23:4 NLT).

"He gives power to the weak and strength to the powerless" (Isaiah 40:29 NLT).

"But those who trust in the Lord will find new strength. They will soar high on wings like eagles. They will run and not grow weary. They will walk and not faint" (Isaiah 40:31 NLT).

"For I hold you by your right hand—I, the Lord your God. And I say to you, don't be afraid. I am here to help you" (Isaiah 41:13 NLT).

"For this is how God loved the world: He gave his one and only Son, so that everyone who believes in him will not perish but have eternal life" (John 3:16 NLT).

"And this same God who takes care of me will supply all your needs from his glorious riches, which have been given to us in Christ Jesus" (Philippians 4:19 NLT).

"If you need wisdom, ask our generous God, and he will give it to you. He will not rebuke you for asking" (James 1:5 NLT).

"So humble yourselves before God. Resist the devil, and he will flee from you" (James 4:7 NLT).

"But if we confess our sins to him, he is faithful and just to forgive us our sins and to cleanse us from all wickedness" (1 John 1:9 NLT).

I could go on and on, but you get the point. The Bible is overflowing with promises and blessings. **Research** them. **Write** them down. **Repeat** them to yourself regularly. Fill your heart and mind with these biblical promises to build up your faith. Claim them as your own.

2. God Chose a Specific Family Genealogy

What kind of family were you born into? In my family, we have multiple generations of pastors. My great-grandfather, my grandfather, and my father were pastors. My brother, David, is a pastor. My husband and I also are involved in ministry.

At the beginning of the twentieth century, my great-grandfather traveled around the world three-and-one-half times spreading the message of the baptism of the Holy Spirit. He wanted to take this message to the world. He was a pioneer missionary. He understood his God-given call and refused to be stopped. He was tireless to fulfill what God had called him to do. This encourages me to press on no matter the cost.

Ask God to put your inheritance through the filter of the Blood of Jesus to give a pure stream of what you should carry. I never imagined that there were so many gifts, talents, and blessings in my family tree. Prophetic and pastoral gifts, teaching and preaching gifts just waiting to be stirred up and used. What positive qualities is your family known for? What does

God want you to develop and pass on? Which ones need to be washed by the Blood of Jesus before you can discern what to do with them?

3. God Was Intentional About Your Ethnic Background

What is your ethnic background? Each ethnic group brings different specialty gifts to the Body of Christ. No one ethnic group represents the multiple facets of God. Together we display the fullness of God. The Book of Revelation pictures the beautiful diversity (nation, tribe, people, language) and unity of the flash mob in Heaven:

> After this I saw a vast crowd, too great to count, from every nation and tribe and people and language, standing in front of the throne and before the Lamb. They were clothed in white robes and held palm branches in their hands. And they were shouting with a great roar, "Salvation comes from our God who sits on the throne and from the Lamb!" (Revelation 7:9-10).

Filter out the extremes and focus on the gifts of your people group. Ask God to show you what is unique to you because of the "tribe" through which He chose to have you born.

Rick Joyner affirms,

> The God we seek to serve loves diversity so much that He made every snowflake different, every tree different, and even every leaf on every tree different. He made us all different. He made all the tribes and cultures in the earth different as a source of constant wonder and marvel. Being free of racism is more than just not thinking evil of those who are different, but it is celebrating and appreciating our differences. ("Rick Joyner's Word For the Week," Week 42, 2003, https://www.morningstarministries.org/resources/prophetic-bulletins/2013/understanding#.W4LDUC2lmP8)

Joyner adds,

God has given great gifts to each ethnic group so that it can be a blessing to all of humanity.

So what I am about to share are generalizations which are not true of everyone in the groups I will talk about. We also need to keep in mind that what may now be weaknesses in any person or group will likely become strengths, once they have experienced the redemption of God.

As stated, God has given special gifts to different ethnic groups. You have to be blind both physically and intellectually to not realize that God has given rhythm to Africans which exceeds that of any other ethnic group, especially those who are of white, European descent. However, some of the best dancers in the world are from white, European descent. Likewise, some of those of African descent that I know have as little rhythm as I do.

A friend of mine who is a music historian pointed out that every musical instrument has its roots in Africa, even those listed in the Bible. Many of these have been greatly changed, revised, and modernized in other cultures, but you can find the origins of every one of them in Africa. Africans tend to have remarkable gifts for music that have blessed the world. This also is translated into a remarkable devotion to worship.

It also seems that, in general, Africans tend to grasp and understand the spiritual realm much faster and easier than those of European descent. This is one of the greatest gifts of all, and has therefore been under a terrible assault of the devil seemingly from the beginning. Some of the strongest witchcraft in the world is found in Africa, or where Africans are the dominant ethnic group in a country. Africa is now experiencing one of the greatest revivals in the world, and we can expect this great gift to result in some of the most powerful healing, deliverance, prophetic, and worship ministries to come out of Africa. Missionaries are about to be sent from Africa throughout the world that the entire body of Christ will be blessed by.

Europeans, in general, tend to be more pragmatic, which can make them great engineers and scientists, historically, and greatly surpassing other cultures in this area. However, some of the world's greatest engineers and scientists have been from African descent. Likewise, some of the world's greatest composers have been from European descent. The African scientists have been able to see things others did not often see because they were not afraid to bring spiritual truths and insight into the laboratory. Likewise, European composers reached unprecedented heights by bringing mathematical precision and even engineering principles to their compositions. ("Rick Joyner's Word For the Week," February 23, 2004, https://www.morningstarministries.org/resources/word-week/2004/healing-nations#.W4LIBC2lmP8)

What might the strengths of different ethnic backgrounds be? My ethnic background is predominantly Italian on my mother's side, and I seem to have inherited many of her qualities. This make me an outsider when looking at many other ethnic backgrounds. That being said, may I submit that it seems that African Americans tend to have a natural rhythm inside of them and have richly blessed the church with music. Chinese are often entrepreneurial. Jews are often excellent money managers. What about you? Are you carrying any keys because of your ethnic background?

In the spring of 2018, the world watched the royal wedding of Prince

Harry and Meghan Markle. Could you have imagined a black Gospel choir singing at a British royal wedding? Meghan embraced her ethnic background and therefore her royal wedding joined more than a man and a woman in matrimony. Meghan, who is half black and half white, was the bridge that connected two radically different worlds to each other. Perhaps the staid British were stretched. Perhaps the Gospel choir was stretched. Perhaps God will stretch you as you come together with other Christians from ethnic backgrounds far different than your personal comfort zone. God knows what He is doing.

4. Your Church Experiences

In what religious background were you raised? Were you raised Catholic with a deep awe and reverence for God and the church? Were you raised Evangelical building into your foundation a profound appreciation for the study of the Bible? Were you raised Pentecostal valuing presence-based worship and a hunger for the supernatural? Did you have no church background until you became an adult? What benefits do you carry from these experiences? What hurts need to be healed because of these experiences? Do you understand the Kingdom principle—**We Can Be Better Together**?

What part does God want you to play not only in your church, but also in His Kingdom? As you live out your part, how is your city more like His heaven? Remember that Jesus prayed, "your will be done, on earth as it is in **heaven**" (Matthew 6:10). Perhaps we should bring this to a more personal level and pray for God's will to be done "in my city" or "in my neighborhood" as it is in heaven.

5. In What Geographic Region Were You Born or Have You Lived?

What city, state, nation? Why in the world did God choose to have you born wherever you were born? Why did God put you in this city at this exact time in human history?

I ask myself, "Why did God take our family from New York State to Chicago to Hong Kong to Missouri, and finally back to New York State?" I believe He had a purpose, but I will probably never know all His reasons. I do know that I have picked up credentials everywhere my feet have settled. Because God has you in a place for His purposes, the ground on which you stand is sacred soil.

"… Wherever you set foot, you will be on land I have given you" (Joshua 1:3 NLT).

6. The Meaning of Your Name

What does your name mean? Was there a reason you were given that name? Have your parents shared why they chose your specific name?

Call forth the characteristics and prophetic purposes of your name.

My brothers both have two middle names: Daniel *James Roderick* Smith and David *John Richard* Smith. For me, my parents only gave me one middle name: Deborah *Jean*. When I asked why, they said it was because one of my grandmother's names was Ruth and the other Rose. They didn't want to offend either mother so I have a single middle name. Even in naming me, my parents didn't want to dishonor the family—a worthy reason.

Years ago, Cindy Jacobs who did not know me at the time called me out of a congregation and declared, "Your name is Deborah! And you will speak the Word of the Lord!" Of course I knew who Deborah was in the Bible—prophet, judge, and worshiper. The Lord used Cindy to prompt me to apply that meaning to my life. What about your name?

7. Personal Prophetic Words

What has God spoken over you and your family? Have there been prophetic words spoken that you can't forget, words for which you have warred? What treasure does God have waiting for you to claim and build on? Prophesy words of blessing and life over your today and tomorrow! Ezekiel looked over a valley of dry bones. God commanded him to prophesy not what he saw (death), but Life, Life, Life.

> "So I prophesied as he commanded me, and breath entered them; they came to life and stood up on their feet—a vast army" (Ezekiel 37:10 NIV).

Mine the treasures in these seven areas of blessings:

- biblical promises;
- family genealogy;
- ethnic background;
- church experiences;
- geographic region (city, state, nation);
- the meaning of your name; and
- personal prophetic words.

You will be amazed at the gems that are waiting to be discovered and uncovered. Start now and tomorrow you will begin to look at yourself differently. With the Psalmist I declare that your strength will be renewed like the eagle.

> "Praise the Lord, my soul; all my inmost being, praise his holy name. Praise the Lord, my soul, and forget not all his benefits— who forgives all your sins and heals all your diseases, who redeems your life from the pit and crowns you with love and compassion, who satisfies your desires with good things so that your youth is renewed like the eagle's" (Psalm 103:1–5 NIV).

Chapter 12

The Healing Hug

SOME OF THE MILEPOSTS ALONG THIS JOURNEY have been painful to uncover. Thankfully, God gives grace for whatever we encounter on the journey. Each milepost has provided an opportunity for healing as I walked this path.

Most of the mileposts have taken me by surprise.  I remember attending a service led by the late Dr. C. Peter Wagner who we had the privilege of knowing for 14 years. A few months earlier, Al and I took Peter out to dinner, sharing an evening of fellowship and laughter. He asked us to share our story, interjecting his wise and insightful thoughts. We were all surprised by how many parallels there were between our stories. We had a memorable evening, feeling blessed that God had given us personal time with a patriarch of the faith.

But the surprise did not come at the dinner months earlier, but in the midst of the crowd at the church service. We arrived early, well before Peter. When Peter came, a group of people gathered to greet him. Unusual for the prim and proper Dr. Wagner, he was a bit disheveled, as his suitcase had not made the flight. He came to speak "as is." After the meeting, we went up to say our goodbyes. Peter said to me, "You didn't give me a hug." He then tenderly wrapped his arms around me and gave me a long fatherly embrace. He held me close, intentionally making the hug last several seconds. Tears came to my eyes. I was surprised at my emotions.

Then came the unexpected twist. The surprise kept going. I couldn't get "the hug" out of my mind. Every time I thought about it, tears literally filled my eyes and ran down my cheeks. Why, I wonder.... Am I that desperate for a father's love?

I look back generationally and recognize that my Grandmother was about 10 years old when her father, Daniel Awrey, died in Africa. I am sure being raised without a father left scars in her. Even though her marriage fell apart, she raised her three children—Esther, Samuel (my Dad), and Grace—with a strong Biblical base, putting God first. But she couldn't undo the hurt caused to my father by being raised without a father.

My father was a great dad, but until later years didn't deal with those childhood wounds. Because of this he chose not to speak about most of his childhood to us kids.

We each carry wounds from our childhood that for whatever reason, even as adults, have not yet been healed. These unhealed wounds affect the way we look at life and live every day. I pray that the life experiences that have given you a certain negative "bent" will be exposed and healed. As I continue to pursue God, He continues to show me hurts and bruises in my spirit that He wants to heal. May God give you grace to walk the road to healing and wholeness so that you can truly carry the pure inheritance that God has prepared for you.

Sometimes I wish I could have a conversation with my Dad who is now in heaven. From up there, he has connected all the dots to what didn't make sense down here. I know he and my mom are cheering me on to go farther and higher and faster than they ever could.

Some of you are frustrated as you read this book. Perhaps you were connect with your biological mother. Others never knew or had relationship with your father.

Since that was not my journey, I do not know your pain, but please allow me to share a thought. Be thankful for the parent or parents you do have. Although parents are never perfect, God used them in your life. Let thanksgiving lead you as you mine for additional generational treasure. Pause and ask your heavenly Father for direction and clues.

Friends of ours adopted a baby girl. Stephen, the father, struggled with the concept of adoption until God showed him that the Father's heart is the perfect expression of adopting kids. This is the reason why we pray, "Our Father, Who art in Heaven.... " We all are kids adopted by our heavenly Father into His ever-expanding family.

So if you are adopted, remember Jesus has added an additional bloodline to you. Someday you may have the privilege of finding out more about your roots, but today recognize that your adoptive parents are God's gift to you.

Remember God promises to be the Father to the fatherless in Psalm 68:5 (NLT): "Father to the fatherless, defender of widows—this is God, whose dwelling is holy."

If one parent raised you, be thankful for the gift of one parent. Research and mine the treasure that is there for you.

As for me, I choose to focus on all the great times we had as a family growing up. If you were to interview my two sons, I hope and pray they would choose the same. Being chained to negative memories produces a bitter root which transfers death, not life. God desires us to cultivate an overcoming spirit that uses even that which was negative to catapult us forward.

My father and mother loved me as best they could, and for that I am very thankful! But for any gap they left, we are truly blessed that God has given us spiritual fathers and mothers who have more than made up the difference. They have affirmed, blessed, encouraged, and corrected us through the years. Specifically, I want to thank God for Tommy and Wanda Reid, Dennis and Katie Wiedrick, Ray Bakke, Pastor and Dr. Hughey, Barbara and Dale Wentroble, and Dr. C. Peter Wagner. (There are so many others who have changed our lives that I can't even count. You know who you are. We thank and honor you.)

For twenty years, Al and I have facilitated a weekly pastors prayer group. These pastors and ministry leaders have become family to us as we have prayed, strategized, and built strong relationships together. A few years after starting the group, one of our spiritual fathers, Dennis Wiedrick, asked to meet with us. We were excited to get together to catch up.

At the meeting, Dennis specifically asked us how pastors prayer was going. We responded, "Great!" He countered by telling us he had received a different report. In a gracious way, he shared that people were saying negative things about how we were running the group. Wow, it was like a knife in our heart. We had given our lives to this group. As the Apostle Paul, we cared for them like family.

> "… we were like a mother feeding and caring for her own children" (1 Thessalonians 2:7 NLT).

How could we be perceived in this way? We asked Dennis, who we knew loved us deeply, what we should do. He suggested that we resign from the group. He said that we needed to respond in the opposite spirit, not defending ourselves, but humbly stepping aside. Although we were heartbroken, we felt he was right so we acted on his word. For three months, we stayed on the sidelines and prayed a blessing on the group. The group kept meeting.

Three months later, we were personally given a letter signed by twelve pastors asking us to facilitate this pastors group on their behalf! This new door came with delegated authority given to us by some of the key gate-keepers of our region. Why do I share this? Sometimes challenging words are spoken over us that God wants to use to transform us, even though in the moment it seems that they will destroy us. God brings fathers into our lives who are able to see the bigger picture. Submitting to fatherly counsel may bring healing to us even though it can be painful to walk it out.

In a way that is hard to comprehend, the words that Dennis gave us were also a **healing hug**. Dennis confronted us because he loved us and because he loved our region. He wanted the best for us.

> "No discipline seems pleasant at the time, but painful. Later on, however, it produces a harvest of righteousness and peace for those who have been trained by it" (Hebrews 12:11 NIV).

We are blessed to have so many friends on the journey with us. If one of us wants to quit, our cheering friends support us through the tough parts of the course. We are also blessed to have physical and spiritual sons and daughters already running ahead of where we were at their age. I heard a saying, "The best way to get an old, arthritic dog up is to buy a puppy!" The *puppies* are yapping at our heels!

What is the role of spiritual moms and dads as the next generation shares the baton? Hodding Carter said it well: "There are two things we should give our children: one is roots and the other is wings." Obviously, we need to help the next generation establish a healthy root system. Roots that go deep, roots that support them through dry times, roots that sustain during heavy winds. A strong root system must be in place to withstand the storms of life.

But roots are not enough. You can admire the root system of a tree, but never lose sight of the wings that will take the next generation higher in the spirit, beyond where we have gone. Wings will raise the next generation to the perspective of the eagle rather than the turkey.

We used to pray primarily for great anointing on our sons. We now pray first for great character in our sons (roots) before God reveals and releases their great anointing (wings).

Now is the time to intentionally pour into the next generation of leaders who are rising among us. We must love, value, affirm, and care for them. When given in love, prayerfully, humbly, and in the right timing, the oil of healing can be poured out all around us.

Early on, Al and I were confused as spiritual parents when we invested personal time and energy into a couple's lives only to have them go in a totally different direction than we had encouraged them to go. How do we handle that? Sometimes better than others. Eventually we learned to try to give them grace as our heavenly Father gives us grace. Let it go. When some day they come face to face with Jesus, He will only ask them how well they obeyed and followed Him, not us. We remind ourselves that His will is perfect for them, while our best wisdom is far from perfect.

(Note: the above is the exception to the rule. Most of those who ask our advice as spiritual parents are a joy with whom to journey. As we have been blessed by those who spoke into our lives, we are blessed by sons and daughters who stewarded whatever thoughts and insights we shared with them and are growing into mature women and men of God.)

As you pray and appropriately pursue authentic relationships, I pray God will connect you to spiritual moms and dads. In addition, I encourage you to be fathers and mothers to younger Christians around you who need extra affirmation and love from a father or mother to be all that they can be. All of us need a father or mother's hug along the way.

May you know the favor of the Lord as He sets you into a nurturing family structure—listening to those to whom you are submitted, walking with those beside you, and nurturing those submitted to you.

"God places the lonely in families; he sets the prisoners free and gives them joy. But he makes the rebellious live in a sun-scorched land" (Psalm 68:6 NLT).

God has blessed us with powerful fathers and mothers to fill the gap. Now it is our turn to do the same. Who needs your life-giving hug today? Are you willing and able to receive a righteous hug from a fellow sojourner? We are Better Together!

Chapter 13

God Sightings

"THE HEAVENS PROCLAIM THE GLORY OF GOD. The skies display his craftsmanship" (Psalm 19:1 NLT).

God is constantly expressing His love to us! As we read the Bible, we can begin to understand how He works. We see how personally and intimately He cares about us. We read seemingly impossible stories of how God communicates to and through His people in supernatural ways.

The Father keeps showing off with "God Sightings"—custom-tailored encounters meant to excite and energize us along the journey. They are meant to awaken things in us that may be part of our inheritance. The whole Bible is full of these "God Sightings."

I like to define these God Sightings as an event that:

1. is unusual
2. focuses our attention on God
3. has a WOW factor
4. surprises us.

God Sightings fill the Bible. Let's interact with a couple with which you are probably familiar. Daniel found himself in the lion's den. Let's be clear. This was not Daniel's Plan A! But the story made the Bible. (Note: some of your least favorite trials have matured you for your God-given assignment, even if they would not have made your Plan A.)

Those lions should have immediately devoured him. But God sent an angel to shut the mouths of the lions because He had an ongoing assignment for Daniel. The King was shocked and overjoyed. The evil men who plotted Daniel's demise were executed.

Dan 6:23-24 (NLT) says: "The king was overjoyed and ordered that Daniel be lifted from the den. Not a scratch was found on him, for he had trusted in his God. Then the king gave orders to arrest the men who had maliciously accused Daniel. He had them thrown into the lions' den, along with their wives and children. The lions leaped on them and tore them apart before they even hit the floor of the den."

Not only were these evil men unable to destroy the prophet of God, but even better King Darius "issued a decree that in every part of my kingdom people must fear and reverence the God of Daniel" (Daniel 6:26a). God won supernaturally!

In a second example, Jonah found himself inside a big fish, definitely not his Plan A. Can you believe that? The fish that Jonah thought would kill him instead saved him! Although Jonah through his disobedience may have caused his predicament, God cared about the call of a man and the destiny of a city. Back on course, Jonah brought revival to Nineveh. A city was saved. God won supernaturally!

A third testimony comes from Joseph who found himself sitting in prison, betrayed and abandoned, certainly not his Plan A. If he had grown bitter and given up on dreams, he would have died in prison. But his accurate interpretation of the Cupbearer to the King's dream brought a delayed invitation from the Pharaoh to interpret his dream.

The tables turned. Joseph—the foreigner, the ex-slave, the ex-con—moved into a very prestigious position of leadership, Vice President of Egypt. God won supernaturally!

In the kind of ironic twist that God enjoys, God tested Joseph to make sure he forgave those in his past who wronged him. Imagine how shocked

Joseph was when his brothers showed up on the scene wanting to buy grain during the famine. He watched as his childhood dreams came to pass in front of his very eyes. And rather than releasing vengeance on his brothers, Joseph fed and blessed them. He knew it had to be God!

Over and over again, we see Jesus supernaturally healing and delivering those who needed His touch. His love was expressed personally to multitudes through these God Sightings. As Jesus spoke, "Anyone who has seen me has seen the Father...." (John 14:9b NLT). I can't imagine how many people were supernaturally touched. Even the Bible states that there was not room to record all the miracles.

> "Jesus also did many other things. If they were all written down, I suppose the whole world could not contain the books that would be written" (John 21:25 NLT)

Jesus won supernaturally!

We cannot forget the Day of Pentecost when God ignited His church. Something began to happen that day that had never happened before, a "God Sighting" that amazed those present and still astounds us today. The fruit of Pentecost continues to bear harvest to this very day. Both the church and the world were changed forever.

> "They were completely amazed. 'How can this be?' they exclaimed. 'These people are all from Galilee, and yet we hear them speaking in our own native languages! Here we are—Parthians, Medes, Elamites, people from Mesopotamia, Judea, Cappadocia, Pontus, the province of Asia, Phrygia, Pamphylia, Egypt, and the areas of Libya around Cyrene, visitors from Rome (both Jews and converts to Judaism), Cretans, and Arabs. And we all hear these people speaking in our own languages about the wonderful things God has done!' They stood there amazed and perplexed. 'What can this mean?' they asked each other" (Acts 2:7-12 NLT).

Could I be so bold to suggest that tightrope walker Nik Wallenda who walked across Niagara Falls was a God Sighting? If you watched the broadcast (along with 20 million others in the international broadcast), Nik prayed out loud to the Father throughout the entire walk high above Niagara Falls. This was a true testimony of a powerful yet out-of-the-box God Sighting. My husband Al called it "taking prayer walking to new heights!"

Time for you to do some work. Personally, have you seen and experienced God sightings? You may say, I'm not important enough for God to notice me. Don't believe that lie from the enemy.

Take a moment now. Pray with me. "Lord, you know times I should have noticed You but I wasn't looking or maybe I have forgotten. Lord, please remind me of God Sightings throughout my lifetime. I want to remember so I can praise You now for Your interventions and encounters that changed my life." Now listen for His response, perhaps a still small voice or impression.

Sometimes it is good to pause and "count your many blessings" as the old hymn suggests. When we understand how God relates to us, we can better share with others by the words of our testimonies.

"And they have defeated him by the blood of the Lamb and by their testimony. And they did not love their lives so much that they were afraid to die" (Revelation 12:11 NLT).

Going beyond the seen God sightings, how many times has He protected us from an almost car accident? If we could only see the angels God has sent to protect us, we would praise God for hidden "God Sightings."

Watch for "God Sightings"! Be alert. Share them! These are your testimonies that defeat the enemy. They build you up and at the same time release hope and encouragement in others. They give strength to press on no matter what we are going through.

My great-grandfather Daniel Awrey wrote dozens of articles for different magazines tracing the global reach of the Azusa Street revival. Al had researched all of Awrey's writings for a research paper he presented for the Society for Pentecostal Studies in 2015. But all the research had not uncovered a single piece of Awrey's personal handwriting. Sadly, by the time we were researching, whatever may have been left after Daniel Awrey died and was buried in Africa in 1913 had long since been thrown away.

Note: God Sighting ahead! In a chance conversation, Al mentioned to Glenn Gohr, great friend and historian, that he had never seen Awrey's handwriting. Glenn connected us with a historian, Cornelis van der Laan, in the Netherlands who kept the hotel register for a guesthouse there. Sure enough, Daniel Awrey stayed there! Van der Laan affirmed,

> Awrey stayed in the home of Gerrit and Wilhelmine Polman in Amsterdam, Kerkstraat 342, just above the Church hall. Awrey wrote in the guest book of the Polmans....

> *"And they were all filled with the Holy Ghost, and began to speak in other tongues as the Spirit gave them utterance." Acts 2:4*
> *"The Blood of Jesus Christ His Son cleanseth us from all sin." 1 John 1:7*
> *Daniel Awrey April 22nd, 1910 Box 416, Hong Kong, China.*

We were thrilled when we received the picture of his handwriting. It brought unexpected joy to our hearts to have this "God Sighting." Even though Daniel Awrey is dead, he lives on. Did you ever consider that when you signed someone's guest book it might outlive you?

The Psalmist sums it up in Psalm 139:16 (NLT): "You saw me before I was born. Every day of my life was recorded in your book. Every moment was laid out before a single day had passed."

But the God Sightings that revolved around Awrey continued for us. We were unprepared for the extent of the adventure when we visited Liberia, the last place in which he ministered and the place where he is buried.

> And they were all filled
> With the Holy Ghost, and
> Began to speak in other tongues,
> As the Spirit gave them utterance
> *Acts 2-4*
> The Blood of Jesus Christ His
> Son cleanseth us from all sin
> *1 John 1-7*
>
> Daniel Awrey
>
> April 22th 1910   Box 416   Hong Kong China

Supernatural surprises filled our journey!

For the first time since we moved to Buffalo, New York, in 1989, we chose to fly out of Toronto instead of Buffalo. Little did we know that fourteen inches of snow would cover the Northeast and close every airport on the East coast on the day we flew. We would have been grounded in Buffalo. But God planned our every step… As we drove to Toronto, it was sunny and clear.

We arrived in Monrovia, Liberia on Friday, February 10th. On Monday, as I was preparing for a message, I suddenly realized that **we had arrived in Liberia,** the place of my great-grandfather Daniel Awrey's death **on what would have been his 148th birthday—Feb. 10th!** We believe God was telling us that we were birthing something new from seeds he planted. This was a powerful "God Sighting" for us. It was also affirming that we were walking in steps ordered by the Lord.

More God Sightings happened as we visited the Flower Pentecostal Heritage Center in Springfield, MO, where our friend Glenn Gohr is the Reference Archivist. This place is full of history of the moves of God around the world. We spent several days researching and making copies of information about Daniel Awrey. We hoped there would be some "God Sightings" for us. And of course there were.

One day, Al told Glenn he would like to know what countries in South America Daniel Awrey had visited. Since Al proposed to me in Peru, the continent of South America holds special interest for us. Glenn didn't know for sure, but he gave Al an old diary from 1913. It was the diary of Alice C. Wood, an Assemblies of God missionary to Argentina. As Al began to read, he suddenly started laughing at these entries:

> *Feb. 5—Daniel Awrey came to our door at four o'clock a.m. and*
> *gave us a great surprise;*

Feb. 8—Some 15 at meeting last night;

Feb. 23—I gave a short message after interpreting for Bro. Awrey in the meeting;

Feb. 24—Brother Awrey left for Chili.

WOW! Supernatural surprise! Imagine that one hundred years from now a relative mining for generational treasure might read your diary and laugh at what you had written about a God encounter!

Another God Sighting centering on Awrey is written by Frank Bartleman in his book, *Around the World by Faith*. Bartleman and Awrey met at Azusa St. years before but didn't know about each other's travels to India. As Bartleman recalls catching a train in India, he reveals,

> … I started to run down the platform to find the third class European car, where I belonged. It was at the rear of the train. I just reached it as the train pulled out. Jumping in I almost fell into brother Daniel Awrey's arms. I had met him once before providentially in the station at Glasgow. Now we stood face-to-face again, without either one having had the slightest idea of the present whereabouts of the other. Here was indeed again the hand of God. Neither of us knew the other was in India. Now I understood why I had had such a strong impression to take the noon train from Madras.…

Imagine in the early 1900's traveling to the other side of the world only to run into an old friend from the USA. This had to be God!! Bartleman and Awrey decided this encounter was a sign from God that they should travel and minister together which they did not only in India, but also in Hong Kong and Shanghai.

God Sightings are always around us if we are looking. I vaguely remembered that an older relative of Al's had a unique name, Fanny Grow. We

had returned to Mountain View High School in Harford, PA, for Al's forty-fifth high school reunion. We were driving through his tiny hometown when out of the corner of my eye I saw a sign and demanded that Al stop and go back. The sign read, "Galusha Grow—Father of the Homestead Act, opening the western lands to free settlement in 1862. Speaker of the House 1861-1863. Returned to Congress 1893-1903. Educated at Franklin Academy, Harford, and buried in this cemetery."

The Grow family was related to Al's Grandpa Stuart. We hadn't even researched his family inheritance, but a God Sighting sent us down a new trail of generational inheritance. Remarkably, one of the first careers that Al wanted to pursue was politics, but his Grandpa discouraged him by telling him that he couldn't be a Christian and a politician.

Was there a piece of politics in Al's inheritance? It gets better. As we researched Galusha Grow, we found out what an outside-the-box leader he was. He started his political career as a Democrat, but as the Congress was voting for slave and free states, Grow was frustrated and became a Republican. There was actually a brawl between northerners and southerners on the floor of Congress in 1858 (Wikipedia refers to "the Congressional Brawl of 1858) after Galusha was called a "Black Republican Puppy" for his support of the African-American slaves.

Grow served as Speaker of the House under Abraham Lincoln. After the Civil War, he wanted even more change than his fellow Republicans so he started a group called the Radical Republicans. This group advocated for voting rights for newly freed slaves, and even considered taking voting rights away from slave owners.

Why am I sharing this history? It is amazing that Al, a descendent of the reformer Galusha Grow, has poured himself into countless areas of justice advocating for blacks and the poor. Were these credentials that were earned years ago by Galusha Grow?

God has opened the door for us to work across racial lines. Could Al carry generational credentials to work in racial reconciliation because of the blood, sweat, and tears shed by Grow?

What's that in your genes? What credentials do you already possess because of battles fought and wars won generations ago? What are you meant to carry and what should you lay down? Watch for "God Sightings" that pop up to remind you of keys that you carry.

Throughout your life, God intends to show you constant "God Sightings." Look for them daily, knowing that some days may reveal several. Journal God Sightings to chronicle them for you and generations to come. Keep your eyes and ears open and God will continually show Himself to you in surprising and creative ways.

"No eye has seen, no ear has heard, and no mind has imagined what God has prepared for those who love him" (1 Corinthians 2:9 NLT).

Chapter 14

Your Legacy

PICTURE A LAWYER'S OFFICE WITH A FAMILY gathered. What might be happening? Perhaps a relative's will is about to be read. Do you have a will? Have you ever been recorded in someone's will? Do you have anything you are specifically leaving as an inheritance to your family? Of course you do! You can't take anything with you! Let me tell you.... YOU ARE LEAVING EVERYTHING HERE!! But what legacy—good or bad—are you leaving behind? If you are like most people, you will leave a mixed legacy. In fact, most of us wish we could do over some of what we said or did, or what we wish we had said or done. Do you have unresolved issues that should be dealt with? Are there relationships that could be better? How will you be remembered long after you are gone?

Our wills include our directions about where our earthly possessions will go. But we are also leaving a spiritual legacy that cannot be written down. Earlier in this book, I spoke about carrying the mantle of my great-grandfather, Daniel Awrey. He traveled around the world and visited five continents. He ministered to missionaries, leaders, and pastors. I find it fascinating that Al and I have also ministered on five continents. We work with business leaders, government leaders, pastors, and more. Could I be carrying a spiritual inheritance that came down from great-grandpa?

Daniel Awrey died in Liberia, West Africa, at age 43 years. He left no money and very few earthly possessions, but he left a powerful legacy of impacting the world based on his deep passion for God no matter the cost. I hope I'm willing to do the same.

Recently, we received word of a tragedy that happened to a long-time friend and mentor, Dr. Ray Bakke. We got to know Ray and Corean in the

1980s when we lived in Chicago. Ray was Al's seminary professor and his wife was an accomplished concert pianist. They had two sons: Woody and Brian. One day their son, Woody brought his African-American friend, also named Brian, home from school. Brian was homeless and eventually the Bakke's adopted him. That meant the Bakke family had two sons named Brian: "Black Brian" and "White Brian."

Flash forward several decades. We were invited to a grand anniversary celebration for Ray and Corean's 80th birthdays. But three days before this special event, their son, Brian Davis Bakke (Black Brian) died suddenly of a stroke. He was 57 years old.

We received the following:

> … The tribute concert we'd long planned, will go on this Sunday with the inclusion of Brian in that tribute. It's a great fit. The very music we will hear is the black sounds of New Orleans in the Banjo, which Corean used to play and lecture about. For 42 years we had the privilege of looking at the world through lenses that Brian influenced. When he was born in 1961, a month before our son Woody who brought him into our family, black people could not vote in fourteen states in the USA.
>
> He came into our family, four grades behind, and hardly able to

read after years on the street. Corean went to all of his teachers at the school to arrange ways for him to catch up, so as to keep his eligibility for sports, and it worked. He graduated with Woody, and went on to college, and led that team to the national finals in their small college basketball tournament. He graduated. He served proudly in the US Army and became a social worker the rest of his life.

Brian Davis had brought the African-American culture into the predominantly Norwegian Bakke family tree. Brian Davis's life was changed forever as was the whole Bakke family. Decorations changed at the big anniversary celebration....

> They will have black and white balloons on our highway sign to mark our driveway for those who come to the program. Black and white, for the keys on the piano and for the black and white family; especially the black and white Brian's.

What legacy are you leaving behind? How much have you touched and changed your world? Brian Davis was a street kid who carried an ethnic DNA that immediately and forever changed the family of which he became a part.

The Bible speaks about inheritance:

> "So now, with God as our witness, and in the sight of all Israel—the Lord's assembly—I give you this charge. Be careful to obey all the commands of the Lord your God, so that you may continue to possess this good land and leave it to your children as a permanent inheritance" (1 Chronicles 28:8 NLT).

Abraham's wife, Sarah had something to say about the family inheritance:

> "But Sarah saw Ishmael—the son of Abraham and her Egyptian

servant Hagar—making fun of her son, Isaac. So she turned to Abraham and demanded, 'Get rid of that slave woman and her son. He is not going to share the inheritance with my son, Isaac. I won't have it!' This upset Abraham very much because Ishmael was his son" (Genesis 21:9-11 NLT).

Whether or not Sarah wanted to pass on the family inheritance to Ishmael did not matter. Bloodlines continue whether we like it or not.

Alfred Nobel was a Swedish chemist, engineer, inventor, businessman, and philanthropist. He is known for inventing dynamite. When his brother died, the newspaper mistakenly printed Alfred's obituary condemning him as a "merchant of death." He was so hurt by this accusation that in his will he set aside money to establish the Nobel Peace prize.

Since March 1901, it has been awarded annually (with some exceptions) to those who have 'done the most or the best work for fraternity between nations, for the abolition or reduction of standing armies and for the holding and promotion of peace congresses. ("Alfred Nobel," Wikipedia, https://en.wikipedia.org/wiki/Alfred_Nobel)

Alfred had the rare opportunity to dramatically change the way his name would be remembered long after his death. How different a legacy he left behind because he chose to! When a person passes away, they take nothing with them … everything is left behind. It's too late to change anything. But as long as you are still breathing, you can change your legacy.

After her death, we were cleaning out Al's Aunt Betty's home. We gave away and threw away things that could have had great worth to her. Aunt Betty probably had stories behind the possessions that filled her home, but she left all that behind. But even the best of her earthly possessions, including the money she left us in her will, pale in comparison to her love for her Jesus that she deposited in all of us. Her spiritual legacy lives on.

One day I came across something very dear to me, my first-born son, Caleb's first hat. That's right! It was the tube stocking with a blue ribbon that was immediately placed on Caleb's head to keep him warm right after his birth. Why did I keep it? It is precious to me. It brings special memories back to me, including the joys of my first pregnancy, giving birth for the first time, holding this little one in my arms, the miracle of birth, the snowstorm that Al drove home in, and so much more. Actually, neither Al nor Caleb could care about this little hat. If I were to die today, they might say, "Why in the world did she keep this hat?" They would probably throw it out. But my family can never throw out my lifetime of prayers for them, my prophecies over them, my belief in them. Prayers never evaporate. They produce fruit for generations to come.

> "… I lavish unfailing love for a thousand generations on those who love me and obey my commands" (Ex. 20:6 NLT).

What are you leaving behind both physically and spiritually? What legacy are you leaving to the next generation(s)? Like Alfred Nobel, would you change that legacy if you still had time? You do. Start today.

When King David knew he was about to die, he wrote what might be considered his last will and testament to be followed after his death. He spoke directly to his son, Solomon, who had just been anointed king.

> "As the time of King David's death approached, he gave this charge to his son Solomon: 'I am going where everyone on earth must someday go. Take courage and be a man. Observe the requirements of the Lord your God, and follow all his ways. Keep the decrees, commands, regulations, and laws written in the Law of Moses so that you will be successful in all you do and wherever you go. If you do this, then the Lord will keep the promise he made to me. He told me, If your descendants live as they should

and follow me faithfully with all their heart and soul, one of them will always sit on the throne of Israel'" (1 Kings 2:1-2 NLT).

All that sounds so positive. But King David had more to say. Imminent death also brought regrets for things he felt he had not finished well, including specific direction for King Solomon to follow after his father's death.

"And there is something else. You know what Joab son of Zeruiah did to me when he murdered my two army commanders, Abner son of Ner and Amasa son of Jether. He pretended that it was an act of war, but it was done in a time of peace, staining his belt and sandals with innocent blood. Do with him what you think best, but don't let him grow old and go to his grave in peace. Be kind to the sons of Barzillai of Gilead. Make them permanent guests at your table, for they took care of me when I fled from your brother Absalom. And remember Shimei son of Gera, the man from Bahurim in Benjamin. He cursed me with a terrible curse as I was fleeing to Mahanaim. When he came down to meet me at the Jordan River, I swore by the Lord that I would not kill him. But that oath does not make him innocent. You are a wise man, and you will know how to arrange a bloody death for him" (2 Kings 2:5-9 NLT).

2 Kings tracks how wisely or not so wisely King Solomon handled these specific situations.

Stop right now. Pause, pray, and reflect. Ask the Lord to show you your legacy as it exists today. Repent if it is not what God intends it to be. Ask for His help to make better choices to create a lasting legacy. Don't wait until your deathbed! Do it today. Change course. Love God. Love neighbors. Reconcile with friends and family. "Don't worry about anything; instead, pray about everything" (Phil. 4:6 NLT).

Begin today, and tomorrow will record your changes. You may even rewrite your will. But more importantly, you will create a righteous legacy that will allow your children to run faster, jump higher, and surpass you in their spiritual race. The unresolved regrets of the preceding generation will not slow them down or trip them up. Your choices today will impact their race tomorrow. Perhaps the generations before you handed you a dirty baton soiled with generational sin. You can do better.

May the Lord give you grace and wisdom to clean up the family baton before you hand it off. Your family tree is depending on you. FINISH WELL!

Chapter 15

Dealing with the Muck

THIS WAS A HARD CHAPTER TO WRITE. I had an internal debate—should I shine a light for all to see on the not-so-pretty parts of my family tree?

In my research and travels to recover my family inheritance, I seldom thought of it as hard work. God always seemed to stir excitement in me as I began to follow a new lead. But as all of you recognize, there are things in our family history that are painful, sinful, shameful, disgraceful.... This is what I refer to as MUCK. The dictionary defines muck as "dirt, rubbish, or waste matter."

No one's personal history is pure and spotless. Even Jesus had "muck" in His family lines, including Rahab the harlot (Matthew 1:5) and other scandalous ancestors, so He understands muck. Thankfully, He came to clean up my muck, your muck, and the muck of the world. I can't emphasize enough that we need to put our muck under the Blood of Jesus and be cleansed. I hear you asking, "how do I release the memory? Do I just stop talking about it? Do I not share it with others? Do I just try and forget it?" When I study my family tree, what is important to hang on to and what is important to cover with the Blood and release? What sows seeds of hope and life and what sows seeds of death and despair?

People, including my ancestors, are a mixed bag. Even the best have tripped up along the way. We are humans with a fallen nature. Family members may have responded in a specific way because of their theology, beliefs, or just the traditions at that point in history. They may not have broken the law, but as we uncover the choices our relatives made, we may wish they had handled things differently. Worse yet, some of them did break the law and paid the price along with their family.

Of course, every family member has an opinion on the family tree. Some are very adamant about what they believe to be right. They express themselves very strongly and fight back when we question if they are right or not. Others are more passive. The four writers of the Gospels write from different perspectives and angles on the numerous adventures that they shared. Even the birth of Christ is voiced from each writer's unique perspective. Sounds like my family reunion!

As my husband and I have walked out the calling on our lives, we have tried to learn when it is best to keep quiet. This is harder for me than Al. Opinions about politics, theology, and even wine consumption are intensely stated. Who is right? On which issue? Is anyone always right? Some seem to think so. Can anyone interpret the Bible totally objectively? Aren't we all influenced by our life experience and culture?

The same is true as I interpret my generational inheritance. As I dug into the history of our family, I was shocked to hear dueling perspectives. My Aunt Esther and my father grew up with a very abusive father. Their sister, Gracie, was eleven years younger, so most of her childhood memories were formed after Grandpa Smith had left the family. Although the following quotes from Aunt Esther may seem long, I encourage the reader to hear the pain that muck can continue to release long after a family member is dead. (Note: I wish I could erase this chapter and pretend it never happened):

> *I don't know how much Sammy [my dad] told you about his father. But I have an admitted bias..... And Gracie—who as a toddler only*

knew her daddy as a man who visited periodically and brought her presents—has no such hang-ups....

My aunt, Esther Brinkley, penned "A Brief Biographical Sketch from a Daughter's Perspective" about my grandfather:

Ernest Charles George Smith was born December 17, 1904, in Pennsylvania, of German descent. Ernest graduated from Pacific College about 1926 (a Free Methodist college in Los Angeles....). Ernest excelled in debate, singing, and was active on a gymnastics team. He planned to enter the ministry.

After he married Ruth Awrey in 1927, he preached regularly at several L.A. missions. Then they traveled back East where he preached briefly at churches in Alabama and Virginia, before they returned to Los Angeles.

Ernest continued preaching in L.A. missions until he joined the Pilgrim Holiness Church, taking a pastorate in San Diego, which lasted less than a year, before returning to L.A.

Ernest's marital infidelity began.... [I, Deb, edited some muck out.]

Ernest's extreme physical abuse of his children.... [I, Deb, edited more muck out. To give context to the reader, my grandmother was a devout Christian who held the biblical view, "Wives, obey your husbands" no matter what.]

Back to Esther's writings:

One of my last beatings resulted in "Daddy" leaving our family for the first time: she [Mother] finally had the courage to defy him! She courageously spoke up that time, saying he would have to stop "strap-ping" me! So he deserted our family while we lived in Westminster, California, as she had not been "obedient" and had interfered with his need to "break my spirit."

Later on, after they resolved their differences, we moved briefly back to L.A.... Sammy and I had been to nine schools in eight years. Mother said we had a right to stay in one place for a while! So Daddy took our car and every cent in Mother's purse (including her tithe) and deserted us in a motel in Chandler, without any food, transpor-tation, or a nickel to make a phone call. But because of a miracle, we were able to get back to L.A. The motel owner, a Christian lady whose family had been converted by Daniel Awrey many years ear-lier, held a yard sale—and bought most of Mother's few belongings herself. This gave us enough for bus-fare to get back to Grandmother Ella Awrey's home in L.A.

Mother was the heroine of Sammy's, Gracie's, and my story: First, she got a secretarial job opening and answering letters for Charles Fuller (of the "Old Fashioned Revival Hour" radio fame, and co-founder of Fuller Theological Seminary). Then she rented a little house to move our family to Alhambra so we could attend Bethany Church (which had a large youth group). And later on, she doubled her salary from $40. a week to $80. a week as a "cherry riveter" at Douglas Aircraft in Long Beach, while working the graveyard shift during the war. After the war, Mother got a job as an inspector for Thermador heat-ers, and saw to it that all three of us children completed college—two of us before there was any such thing as "government loans."

Meanwhile, Daddy and Mother reconciled periodically over the next six or so years. He worked as a purser on board the Grace Lines that shipped supplies around the world. He would come home for a while, but would never contribute a cent to our family's expenses, even when he had money, while Mother continued working. After each time he left, she would accept him back when he returned, always believing things would be different—until he decided to leave again.

Finally, after a number of years of his arriving home with promises, then leaving again after several months, Mother announced when he said he was leaving again: "Ernest, if you leave this time, I will never accept you back again." He left anyway. And a few months later she kept her word, refusing to allow him to stay, when he came back home again, broke and out of work.

In angry, bitter letters that she let me read, he vowed that she would be sorry! To get even with her, he stole a U.S. Mail truck and drove it over state lines, then walked into a police station in Texas, and said: "I have committed a federal offense. Put me in prison." After a psychiatric examination, they obliged him. In repeated, rambling accusations in his many letters to Mother, Sammy, and me, he blamed each one of us for his failures and for the breakup of our family.

After being assigned as the "librarian" of the prison, and becoming a member of the "Christian Brotherhood" of inmates, Daddy died of a heart attack in a federal penitentiary in Texas in 1961. (He had asked to return to prison from parole, saying he was too sick to work.) In a final letter to Sammy, he partially accepted the responsibility for deserting his family, but still blamed Mother.

Later, Esther sent this to me:

Whereas prison authorities judged him "sane," psychologists would undoubtedly describe him as emotionally disturbed. Upon knowing the whole, true perspective of the man, psychiatrists would probably call him a "split personality."

My gut feelings are this: If someone were to ask me if I ever knew anyone who I thought had become "demon possessed"—I would answer, "Yes, my father." However, years ago, in my second year of college, after a long prayer session, I wrote to him, completely forgiving him. And a great weight lifted, unshackling me and allowing me from that time on to become the person that God had created me to be. Bravo for forgiveness!"

Was that as hard for you to read as it was for me to write? OK, tell the truth. You are surprised at how unsanctified I am, aren't you? My family tree is crazier than even I expected. My grandfather was both a pastor and a felon. Does your tree look better or worse? The Bible is filled with crazy family trees. The first family, Adam and Eve, had one son that murdered another son. Quite the beginning to humankind. But that is where redemption comes in. Emphasizing Aunt Esther's summary of her dysfunctional family—**BRAVO FOR FORGIVENESS!** You cannot choose your family tree, but you can choose how you **respond** to your family tree.

Because of the failings of my grandfather, Ernest Smith, he became

a scarecrow in my life. Although I never met him, he influenced my life. Family members seldom spoke of him except in a negative light. As I mentioned in a previous chapter, he earned the "black sheep" reputation for our family. It would be unfair, actually impossible, to erase him from my generational inheritance. Although they were not talked about, I'm sure Ernest had good qualities as well as bad. Whether I like it or not, I carry his bloodlines. Ernest gave me practice in praying the Blood over my family tree.

So why did I include this "muck"? My Dad was a pastor for many years, but because of his harsh childhood, he was unable to help others in certain situations because he had never dealt with his own childhood wounds. I remember as a young girl my father attending a school of pastoral care led by Agnes Sanford. My father had a recurring memory from one of the times his father left the family. His dad and he were walking down the sidewalk. My dad was carrying his father's suitcase on the way to the train. His father, a grown man, was shouting all kinds of curse words at my dad, blaming him for the hurt, pain, and separation of the family.

In a private prayer session, Agnes Sanford prayed that my dad would see this traumatic experience through God's eyes. As they prayed, once again my dad found himself walking down the sidewalk carrying his father's suitcase. His father was yelling the same painful accusations, but this time there was a difference. Through God's eyes, my dad saw himself as a full-grown man, while his dad was a small child yelling at the top of his lungs. This was a game-changer. My dad could forgive the words of an ignorant child. During this healing time, my dad was able to release and forgive his father.

When my father returned home after this healing experience, he was never the same again. A sweeter side of my father began to show through. His pastoral ministry grew deeper as he was able to walk many others through the healing of their deep-seated, hurtful memories. Although it was a process, as an adult my dad was able to heal from numerous childhood hurts. Maybe God can teach an old dog new tricks.

As you read about my grandmother through the writing of Aunt Esther, you may see her as an enabler to her husband. But you would miss so much of the God in her. I remember Grandma as a powerful overcomer. In spite of all the odds, she created a godly atmosphere and raised three children who followed Christ. I thank God for the difference she made in my life.

Do you have some muck from your immediate family or from generations farther back? God can heal memories. God wants to heal memories. I agree that some dirty family laundry should never be spoken of again, but other parts of a tainted past are meant to push you into your destiny as the overcomer you are called to be. I suggest you only dig up old family muck if it is bearing current bad fruit. Anything that continues to bear bad fruit should be dealt with using spiritual warfare techniques.

I pray that my vulnerability in this chapter allows you to find new freedom on your journey. Seek God and you will find the grace and healing power needed in your own life. Don't let your memories cripple you, but force you to draw closer to Him. I also recommend seeking out gifted Christian counselors who will help walk you through this healing process. Christian counselors gave me insight I was not getting on my own. Healing and restoration are worth the effort.

Remember the last word from Aunt Esther — **BRAVO FOR FORGIVENESS!**

If there is "muck" in your family tree, pray this prayer with me:

Lord, You have positioned me in this family. I see some of the "muck" that is there. You see it all. I ask that You would cover all of it with Your blood. Cleanse my family tree. Breathe in new life to the tree. Help me to see those painful and traumatic memories through Your eyes. And give me the ability to completely forgive as You have forgiven me. I CHOOSE to forgive. In Jesus' Name, AMEN.

Chapter 16

Funeral Home Visit

We walked into the funeral home surprised that we were the only ones there. The funeral director informed us that the hours for visitation were over, but invited us to go in and say our goodbyes. The woman lying there was a well-known evangelist, Rev. Velma Jones. She touched the lives of many, including Bishop T.D. Jakes, a well-known pastor, author, filmmaker, and Bishop of The Potter's House in Dallas, TX.

We felt honored to be standing at the casket of a woman who had significantly changed the world forever. Of course, she had already gone to her heavenly reward. Was there a reason we were alone with this precious saint of God? Could there be promises God made to Mother Jones that might be fulfilled by us? She carried a mothering mantle that extended all over the country. Was there a puzzle piece to pick up?

We quietly and reverently stood there, feeling the weight of the moment. We then agreed that we didn't want any part of her "mantle" to fall to the ground without fruit. We prayed and claimed any part of her "mantle" that was meant by God for us to carry.

I don't know what we received that day. Mother Jones wasn't a blood relative, but she was in our spiritual family tree as a member of the family of God. We were open to receiving anything our Father had for us that day. (Note: as we were advised by a wise spiritual father, we ran this mantle through the blood of Jesus before we received it. Nothing less, nothing more, than all He wants for us.)

Death is a strange thing. We talk about heaven, we sing about heaven, we watch movies about heaven, we say we want to go to heaven. But when the time arrives, we fight to the last breath to stay here and are reluctant to release our loved ones who are in Christ.

A close personal friend, Virginia (not her real name), was dying of cancer. I wish you had known Virginia, a powerful woman who impacted our region through her love and support for the unborn. She loved God and loved people. She had a gift of connecting people who were stronger together. I can't count the number of times we prayed for her healing, hoping God would spare her.

The call from her family came early one morning. Virginia was in her last hours at the hospital. We immediately drove there in hopes of seeing her one last time. As we arrived, it was obvious that she had just passed. We waited until the family had said their goodbyes and were ready to leave. We asked if it would be okay for us to say our goodbyes after they left. They graciously agreed.

However, as we were alone with Virginia, more than thoughts of goodbye filled our hearts. This time we had different expectations than previous times in hospital rooms. The Lord had been teaching us to pray supernatural prayers to release signs, wonders, and miracles. Did God want to resurrect and heal our friend? Did God want to raise her from the dead? The thought was invigorating and scary. I looked at Al and said, "What if she comes back to life? What would we tell the family?" Al chuckled and said, "Trust me. They would be excited!"

We started praying. Her body was thin and frail from the cancer. Her hair had thinned. A key we learned that day about praying for a dead person—close your eyes when you pray and ask the Lord to help you see the person through eyes of the Spirit. We prayed through eyes of faith. We then opened our eyes, looking for movement, a rising of her chest, a flicker of an eyelid. Nothing. We closed our eyes and prayed again. We mustered up all the faith we had, but Virginia had already embraced her first love, Jesus. We released her to stay at her new and better home with her perfect body.

You might ask why we would pray over a dead person. Years ago, we attended a Dove Christian Fellowship International pastoral seminar. A speaker asked the attendees if they believed God still healed today. Every hand went up. He asked if we had prayed for sick people and seen them healed. Every hand went up. He asked if we believed that God still raised the dead. Every hand went up. He asked how many of us had prayed for a dead person. Out of the hundreds of attendees, only 3 hands went up.

He challenged us to match our actions with the beliefs we confessed. The Lord convicted us. So we prayed for Virginia, have prayed over others who have died (no supernatural resurrections yet!), and would do it again if prompted by the Holy Spirit.

We walked out of Virgina's room with an experience that we will never forget. We know that death is final, but might Lazarus choose to disagree? The angel of the Lord said to the Virgin Mary, "For with God nothing will be impossible" (Luke 1:37 NKJV). Are you hungry to know and follow the God of the humanly impossible? Let's stop limiting God and keep believing for the impossible.

My dad's relatives lived unusually long lives. Great-Grandma Awrey lived to be 101 years old. As a teenager, I remember seeing her grave and being very impressed—"Born 1867 – Died 1968." Her daughter, Great Aunt Ina, lived to be almost 106 years old. My grandma lived to be in her late nineties. Sadly, my mom died at 70 years of age. Whether our years are lengthy or all too brief, we trust that God orders our steps. We trust Him to give us every day that has been set for us.

Make each day count. Truett Cathy, founder of Chick-fil-A, para-phrased as follows: "I have an imagination that every encounter I have with another human being, however brief, holds within it the potentiality of changing the trajectory of that person's life forever." During your life, whom are you influencing? After your death, who will have had the trajec-tory of their lives changed forever? **God intends the fruit of your life to be alive, healthy, and reproducing long after your death.**

At the ripe age of 100, Great Aunt Ina stood before her church with great spiritual authority, powerfully quoting scripture that she had memo-rized years earlier. She never had any children of her own, so she invested her money in missionaries around the world. Her business card read, "THE MISSIONARY'S FRIEND." Al and I, our children, our grand-children, and lots of other rela-tives are still building on these spiritual giants in our family tree. We are fruit that remains to these "mighty oaks of righteousness" (Isaiah 61:3). The Awrey anointing lives on in our family inheritance.

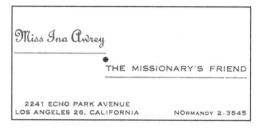

When my husband's mom passed away, she didn't want us to have a funeral. As we stood at the graveside on that wet, gloomy day, our memories extended beyond the open grave to the impact of her life. We remembered the lives she touched through her intercession and through her love. We remembered her love for missions and for her family. We remembered how lovingly she prepared meals for both strangers and friends. She always greet-ed people with a sweet smile and kind words. Her love for God was deep and continues to live through us as well as others whom she influenced.

The most memorable funeral we have ever attended was for a friend, Pastor Fred Naedele, pastor of My Father's House in Elma, NY. People often talk about a funeral being a celebration of life— but Fred's funeral was a CELEBRATION OF LIFE! Just what God-loving and fun-loving Fred would have wanted.

Fred always dreamed outside the box. At a meeting, he wondered out loud if we should drive a pickup truck around the region on a Saturday night, pulling out all the church signs with individual names and replacing them with the identical sign for all—"The Church at Buffalo."

Fred had a heart to see His Church come together and the kingdom of God arise. At his funeral, we laughed, cried, sang, and snuck a peek into heaven where he finally knew how to play the piano! He tried to play down here without much success, but told us one day.... We truly celebrated a saint of God entering heaven.

Funerals are a great time to remember the past, but may we never forget the spiritual inheritance and mantle that is left behind for us to steward. The baton of generations is in your hands. Run well!

Chapter 17

Our Generational Bible

As I was reading my Bible, I had an Aha moment. My great-grandfather read this same book! In fact, generation after generation have read this same book.

The Bible has been loved and reverenced for centuries. In the early Middle Ages, Benedictine **monks hand copied the Scripture** word by word, using quills dipped in ink. These were manuscripts for their own collections, but in so doing, they helped to preserve the Scripture. In the U.S., government officials are still often sworn in with their right hand on the Bible.

The Bible has also been feared and reviled. The Bible has been burned. At times in history, some of them recent, people have died for owning or reading a Bible. In some nations, no one owns a Bible. Each member of the church has memorized a section of the Bible so together they can recite the Bible out loud. Christians have been imprisoned for smuggling Bibles into nations where it is banned. But the Bible has outlived all this.

As a kid, I believed that one day the government would confiscate all our Bibles.... I have so many copies I wouldn't even know where to find them all. My Dad even had the entire Bible on a microscope slide.

If you are like me, you have several copies of the Bible lying around your home. But do you read it? I find it hard to throw away a Bible. Why is that? Is there an emotional attachment? Is there a God-given love for a precious book? But do you read it? It contains the words of life. But do you read it? The Bible is full of promises for us from Genesis to Revelation.

Wikipedia explains, "The **Bible** is a collection of sacred texts or scriptures that Jews and Christians consider to be a product of divine inspiration and a record of the relationship between God and humans." With estimated total sales of over 5 billion copies, it is widely considered to be the most influential and best-selling book of all time.

The **Gutenberg Bible** was the first major book printed using mass-produced movable metal type in Europe. It marked the start of the "Gutenberg Revolution" and the age of the printed book in the West.

Before the Gutenberg press, only the elite had access to the Bible. Only the elite could read. Think how privileged we are to be able to read our own personal Bible. Yet there is such a contrast. Thousands of Bibles are left dusty and unread, while others have been completely worn out because of so much use. For many generations, the family Bible complete with the family tree was passed down from generation to generation, occupying a special spot in the living room, but was seldom if ever read.

The Bible has been preached on, burned, duplicated, translated, loved, hated, and paraphrased. Multiple translations have been penned. Thousands of commentaries and study books have been written. Yet there has always been and still is heated arguing over what it means. The arguments have divided families, churches, and at times nations.

When I was about 7 years old, my Sunday school teacher encouraged our class to memorize the Bible. I took to heart what she said and began memorizing my little New Testament. I started at Matthew 1:1-2 (KJV): "The book of the generation of Jesus Christ, the son of David, the son of Abraham. Abraham begat Isaac; and Isaac begat Jacob; and Jacob begat Judas and his brethren...."

My Dad entered the room and asked what I was doing. I explained to him that my Sunday School teacher, Iola Wickham, had encouraged us to memorize the Bible. He chuckled when he saw me wrestling with the genealogy of Christ and kindly suggested, "Why don't you start with my favorite verses, John 3:16-18." Thanks Dad for redirecting my good intention.

Memorizing Scripture made sense to me, thus beginning my lifetime journey of memorizing "key" verses throughout the Bible. One verse I remember teaching my sons was Psalm 56:3: "But when I am afraid, I will put my trust in You."

I pray that my sons will always take this simple verse to heart. This is one of many Biblical promises that I taught them. I wanted to arm them for spiritual battle in the world as well as instill Scripture as a spiritual legacy for them.

The Bible is a well-preserved generational inheritance for all of us. Every day God wants to use it to bless, guide, direct, and impact our lives. Don't take for granted the treasure given to us. Through the centuries, Christians paid a great price to get it to us. Treat the Bible as more precious than if you had been left ten million dollars of cash as a personal inheritance.

The Word of God is referred to as the sword of the Spirit (Eph. 6:17). Wield it wisely. Wield it often. Study it. Treasure it. The Bible can save your life and the lives of generations yet to be born.

Chapter 18

The Small Vase

IN THE PRECEDING CHAPTERS, I FOCUSED EACH chapter on a large and significant puzzle piece. But as in most of our lives, I have found small puzzle pieces that still proved to be important. Let's look at some of the small puzzle pieces I picked up along the way.

The first was a gift from my Aunt Esther who lives in Lakeside, MT. The car trip to pick up this puzzle piece stretched me, because it was the first time digging for generational treasures that Al was not with me. I did it alone.

Al was taking a doctoral class in Seattle, WA. My Aunt Esther lives in MT. I rented a car and drove over 1000 miles alone through the spectacular mountain terrain. This is not normal for me. Al does most of the driving, but I had such a passion within me to find out more about my family history from my father's older sister that I determined to go for it.

Those few days I spent with my aunt were memorable. As a teenager, our family moved from NY to CA and lived with Aunt Esther for several months until we were able to purchase our own home. At the same time, my aunt was my homeroom and church history teacher at Village Christian School so I saw her a lot.

After moving out, our interaction dropped off to holiday gatherings, family weddings, and funerals. Having grown up with my father, Esther was very revealing about painful family issues. She filled in many of the holes about family history that had been kept from me as a young person. I discovered far more muck than I imagined. Remember to filter through the blood of Christ all that you hear from family members. Hold on to only what is life giving and enriching.

At the end of our time together, I asked if she had something from my great-grandfather that I could have. I wanted something that I could actually touch, something he had held. She gave me a small clay vase with the word "Nazareth" carved into it. Esther told me that her grandfather had brought the vase home from the Holy Land as a gift for his young daughter, my Great Aunt Ina. Although the vase is a simple souvenir, it is incredibly precious to me. It is a connection point with my great-grandfather, Daniel Awrey.

We hoped that some day we would also visit Nazareth. In 2017, we were invited by local Jewish leaders to join them in the Holy Land. While we were in Nazareth, we bought a small memento to remind ourselves that Nazareth is doubly sacred to our family. Al and I took time to pray to pick up any generational inheritance that we were meant to carry. We felt special to walk on the same stones that our family member may have walked on over one hundred years before us.

While in the Upper Room in Jerusalem, we imagined Daniel Awrey spending time praying for God to fill him anew and afresh with the Holy Spirit just as He did to the disciples on the day of Pentecost. We wondered what did Daniel Awrey do when he stood in this room? Who was he with?

What impartation did it leave with him? For centuries, passionate followers of Jesus have made the Upper Room more than a tourist site, but rather a sacred place for Holy Spirit encounter.

As we stood there, a young man approached Al and asked if he was a pastor. The young man said he had recently become a follower of Jesus and asked if Al would pray for him. Al invited several pastors from our group to pray and prophesy over this precious, spiritually hungry young man. How fitting that this room once again became a place of open heaven and spiritual encounter. I wonder if Daniel Awrey ministered to anyone in this space.

Back to the vase. It is just a simple, handmade clay vase, but it has a story. We know that my great-grandfather traveled to the Holy Land in the early 1900's. We know that he loved his daughter enough to buy her this special gift. We know that the vase traveled with him back across the ocean in a ship, possibly even in his pocket. My Great Aunt Ina lived to be almost 106 years old and was a passionate follower of Christ like her father. As her great niece, I recovered a family treasure. But greater than the vase, I carry a rich spiritual inheritance passed down to me.

Have you ever noticed that the Bible is full of lists of family names? For example, Joseph's great-grandfather was Abraham. Boaz's great-grandson was David. In Matthew 1, the gospel writer lays out the lineage of Jesus. Generational lineage is important to God. Perhaps we should pay attention, too. Are there any keys in the generations that have gone before you that God wants you to find and use for your assignment?

Now the second small puzzle piece: a barn door hinge. Remember when we visited the old family farm in Guelph, Ontario, Canada? Geoff Pantling, the current property owner, took us on a tour of the old barn that was built by Daniel Awrey's father in the 1800s. Laying on the barn floor was the original barn hinge that had been replaced when the barn door was upgraded. Geoff reached down and asked if I would like it. I'm still

not sure why I was so excited to say "yes." Perhaps another connection point?

To me, the hinge was a prophetic picture that God was opening wide the doors of provision for me, barn door size. Even as I write this book, I believe God is using this hinge to powerfully encourage you the reader to honor the past and dig up generational keys that are laying around dusty, rusty, and unused. Even gold nuggets in the prospector's pan have to be washed to reveal their worth.

I remember hearing about a dream where someone went to heaven. He saw rooms filled with wrapped packages of various sizes. All these packages sat unopened with no one picking them up. When the person asked, the angel said these were packages of arms and legs and eyes and other body parts waiting for prayers asking for God to miraculously heal today as Jesus did when He walked the face of the earth. Are there any unwrapped packages in heaven waiting for you to request them?

"Until now you have not asked for anything in my name. Ask and you will receive, and your joy will be complete" (John 16:24 NIV).

God wants to fill you with His joy. He wants to give you abundant gifts.

"And God is able to bless you abundantly, so that in all things at all times, having all that you need, you will abound in every good work" (2 Corinthians 9:8 NIV).

A third small puzzle piece came from my Aunt Cassie (Uncle Manny's wife) who knew I was writing a book on recovering a generational inheritance. She kept her eyes open when she was downsizing her home. When she came across a small, yellowed note pad that belonged to Grandpa Buda (my mother's father), she thought of me. The pad was filled with handwritten notes in Italian. I couldn't read it, so I took it to my friend, Joseph. Joseph found what appeared to be notes with Scripture references.

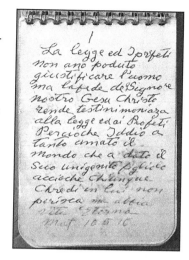

Decades ago, my Grandpa Buda was studying Scripture and writing down his impressions, much as I do today. Perhaps he was preparing sermon notes, but regardless I now have his thoughts on the Bible written by his own hand. Once again, I had recovered a family treasure.

"The Kingdom of Heaven is like a treasure that a man discovered hidden in a field. In his excitement, he hid it again and sold everything he owned to get enough money to buy the field. Again, the Kingdom of Heaven is like a merchant on the lookout for choice pearls. When he discovered a pearl of great value, he sold everything he owned and bought it!" (Matthew 13:44-46 NLT).

In this passage, Jesus explains the Kingdom of Heaven. The Kingdom is a precious treasure, worth everything that we have. God calls us to invest everything to gain it.

Earlier in Matthew, Jesus instructs us to pray, "May your will be done on earth, as it is in heaven" (Matthew 6:10). Imagine the pattern of heaven being reproduced and established on earth. The Kingdom of Heaven is not just someplace we go when we die. It is pattern of living that God wants us to establish as we go about our daily lives on earth. The kingdom is here and now. "… the kingdom of God is within you" (Luke 17:21 NKJV).

Why have I personalized so many of these puzzle pieces? When Jesus walked among us, His sermons were pulled from everything around Him—flowers, trees, birds. Jesus recognized the truth of God hidden in everything. God wants to show us His truth hidden in simple encounters, simple memories, simple truths, and simple objects. God is talking to you all the time in so many different ways. Are you listening? Are you watching for those "God winks"? Pay attention to those tiny moments that God releases a piece of joy that makes you giggle like a delighted child. If the joy of the Lord is supposed to be our strength, then we need to be in touch with our emotions.

Where is your small vase? Where is your barn door hinge? Where is your old tattered notebook? What has God strewn across your path to bring joy to your heart and a giggle to your lips? Ask for eyes to see and ears to hear as He leads you to recover your hidden treasures.

Chapter 19

Curious to Find More

As I began my journey to recover a family inheritance that was buried, I was definitely surprised that hidden behind the scarecrow of my grandfather's transgressions were some magnificent treasures in the previous generation.

But be warned, as you interview family members, dig deep for the truth, not just family gossip and incomplete memories. You may find something you want to be true. Keep digging for supporting facts. What a person tells you may very well be what they believe to be true, but it is only their perspective. It is important to stand on the truth and not just hearsay. You may be desperate to find out more. Some people who dive into their family tree have been known to lose perspective. Be careful.

Mike Bickle tells the story in his book, *Passion for Jesus*, about the time he was desperate to hear direction from God. He and his teenage friend had attended a meeting and wanted to hear whether God wanted them to go to Africa to evangelize the country. They returned to their basement room, which was very dark. They asked God to give them a sign. Suddenly, **a flame appeared**. They were stunned and afraid to move. Unfortunately, it turned out it was just the pilot light on the hot water heater that had suddenly turned on. They didn't go to Africa.... Although this is a funny experience, unbridled enthusiasm can cause us to misread God. As the railroad sign wisely says, "Stop, Look, and Listen." Look for more than a single sign.

When Moses was walking through the wilderness, "There the angel of the Lord appeared to him in a blazing fire from the middle of a bush. Moses stared in amazement. Though the bush was engulfed in flames, it didn't burn up. 'This is amazing,' Moses said to himself. 'Why isn't that bush burning up? I must go see it'" (Exodus 3:2-3 NLT).

In this encounter, it was the right time for Moses to go after what was right in front of him. Hindsight shows us that the bush set Moses up for a complete God redirection of his life. But God gave Moses a series of signs to confirm His presence and direction on the journey.

As you do research, God will surprise you with small nuggets that will be precious to you. Pick each nugget up, look at it, pray over it, ponder if there is a trail to follow, or if it is just a distraction. Even if it doesn't make sense now, you can always keep that puzzle piece in your pocket for a later time.

The wise men in the Bible continually watched the stars looking for signs that prophecy was being fulfilled. What were they looking for? When they saw the famous star in the East around the time of the birth of the Christ child, it triggered a memory of an ancient prophecy about a King being born. Not just an ordinary memory, but one so life-changing that they assembled an entire caravan to follow the leading of the star on a journey that may have taken months or even years. In the words of Tommy Tenney, they were God chasers.

My great-grandfather, Daniel Awrey, was desperate for more of God. He believed there had to be something more to his relationship with Jesus Christ. He would not settle for less. On New Year's Eve 1890-1891, he got down on his knees and told God that he wouldn't get up until he experienced it. Awrey (as quoted by Glenn Gohr) recounts the details....

On the last night of the old year of 1890, Awrey was reading in this book until about a quarter to twelve. Having decided to start the New Year on his knees, he laid down the book, and then he felt the Lord speak to his heart, "There is another experience for you."

Meditating further on what he had read in the book and what he knew to be true from the Scriptures, Awrey was ready for whatever the Lord had in store for him, He told God, "If there is, I am going to have it, and I am going to kneel down her for it, and I will never get up without it." He expected to be there for several hours.

When the whistles began to blow and the bells rang out announcing the New Year, he dropped to his knees and believed and trusted in God to sanctify him wholly in every way possible. A real peace flooded his soul.

The next morning while conducting family worship in the Samuelson home, he felt the anointing of the Holy Spirit in a powerful way. It was like oil being poured throughout: his spirit, soul, and body.

That night, the first night of the new year, he went to prayer meeting, and after calling on several others to pray, the leader asked for voluntary prayer. Awrey reports, "I began to pray and the Holy Spirit prayed through me in another tongue, and by faith the prayer went right up to the throne of God." He says that he saw a flame of fire come down on his head and the Lord took control of his tongue, making him pray in another language. The blessing of God went all through his being. He felt like all three persons of the Trinity had come to dwell in his heart and life in a very real way.

Wow! This was my great grandfather's experience. But as striking as this puzzle piece seems to me today, if I had picked it up early in my journey, it would have meant very little to me. For most of my early life, I did not know about or understand the gift of tongues. Glenn Gohr wrote the article above in 2000, but I didn't discover it until 2006. As this puzzle piece sat hidden from me, God held it for the right time and the right place where I would understand and value my inheritance. In the fullness of time, Glenn's article became a key that opened countless doors to the writing of this book.

Luke focuses on the persistence of the seeker: "And so I tell you, keep on asking, and you will receive what you ask for. Keep on seeking, and you will find. Keep on knocking, and the door will be opened to you" (Luke 11:9 NLT).

If God has something specific for you to uncover in your past, He will give you multiple opportunities to trip over it. He will remind you of it over and over again. He loves you so much He wants you to find and enjoy any "treasures hidden in the darkness" (Isaiah 45:3 NLT).

Are you satisfied? How hungry are you for a deeper relationship with God? Do you want to press on to receive all that God has for you? As you become more desperate to uncover the treasures God has for you, it may drive you to do some wild and crazy things. People have asked why we would go to Canada to look for gravestones. Why would we pray in the Los Angeles plaza where Daniel Awrey preached during the Azusa Street revivals? Why would we return to the Buda family farm in Syracuse? Why pull over to take pictures of an old historical marker in a family cemetery in Al's old hometown in Pennsylvania? Why would we go overseas to Liberia, West Africa, one hundred years after the death of my great-grandfather there? Why? Because like Moses, I saw something unusual and felt, *"I must go see it!"* How about you? Have you heard any burning bushes calling your name recently? As the song reminds us,

We are standing on holy ground
For I know that there are angels all around
Let us praise Jesus now
For we are standing in His presence on holy ground.

Chapter 20

Praying For Your Children

Much of my book has looked back as God focused me on recovering my generational inheritance. But equally important is the view forward as I focus on the next generations. **Passing on a generational inheritance must include regular prayer for your children and grandchildren.** I believe that I am still benefiting from the generations of prayers before me. Prayers that my parents, grandparents, and even great-grandparents prayed continue to impact my daily life. No prayer is ever wasted or forgotten.

> "And when he took the scroll, the four living beings and the twenty-four elders fell down before the Lamb. Each one had a harp, and they held gold bowls filled with incense, which are the prayers of God's people" (Revelation 5:8 NLT).

Can you imagine how many prayers have been prayed for you? Thousands? Tens of thousands? More? Did you remember that Jesus Himself prayed for each one of us?—"I am praying not only for these disciples but also for all who will ever believe in me through their message" (John 17:20 NLT).

I am overwhelmed at this thought. I know I have prayed for people I barely even know. How many golden bowls are there in heaven full of prayers for us? How many golden bowls are there in heaven full of our prayers for others?

Daniel Awrey describes the time his wife and he prayed and anointed his baby with oil to be healed from a high fever. The bowls of prayer tipped earthwards. God healed their son, but the preacher publicly accused Awrey of being a fanatic for not seeing a doctor. I believe you have to be wise. Doctors are sometimes God's answer for healing, but prayer should be the first response, the default switch, for every Christian's need.

Our son, Nathan, was struggling with alcohol abuse while he was in high school. As a mom, I knew there were times that my nagging was worthless and the only place to go was to God in prayer. If Al and I knew the extent of his addiction, we would have been even more concerned, but God hid a lot from us.

Then came the night I will never forget. In the middle of the night, Nathan entered our bedroom sobbing uncontrollably. Even as he sat down beside me, the bed shook. "What's the matter?" I probed. He gasped, "I had a dream!" He began to tell us the dream. He saw a big box at the bottom of the bed and I told him not to touch the box. But he touched the box, which fell off the bed and sprung open. His dead body rolled out and he knew that if he didn't stop drinking that would be him. That night, Nathan was supernaturally delivered and transformed forever!

Later when I asked God why He didn't tell me the extent of Nathan's drinking, I felt He said that my response would have been to ground him or use some sort of punishment that would have been totally useless. Instead, I found my power in the closet, praying for my youngest son. Fighting in the spirit released God to do His supernatural work in Nathan through a God-given dream.

Nathan gave me permission to tell his story. As I have shared his testimony across the world, hundreds have asked me to pray for their prodigals. Where are you today? Are you grieved for your next generation? Are you all prayed and cried out for a prodigal? Don't quit. Your Father loves your child more than you possibly could, and this Father can work in supernatural ways!

Dreams and visions are only a fraction of His net to capture the heart of your next generation son or daughter. I'm praying that these words will encourage you to keep praying and believing. Lord, bring each prodigal to his or her senses. Bring them home to us and You.

Whose prayers were heard and answered that night? Mine? Al's? Nathan's grandparents? Sunday school teachers? Friends? All of the above? It doesn't matter. The bowls of prayer tipped earthward.

It has been said that Christianity is never more than one generation away from extinction. All it takes to lose everything is for one generation to fail to transfer its beliefs and principles to the next generation.

"After that generation died, another generation grew up who did not acknowledge the Lord or remember the mighty things he had done for Israel" (Judges 2:10 NLT).

How do you pass God on to the next generation? Start young. We prayed over our children while they were still in my tummy. Once they arrive, remind them over and over again that God loves and cares for them. Tell them the stories of the Bible. Share your personal stories of God's mighty works on your behalf.

Before our grandson, Caiden was born, Nathan and Megan told us what his name was going to be—Caiden Elijah Warner. I researched the meaning of his name and began to pray for Caiden Elijah Warner while Megan was still pregnant. Caiden means *valiant warrior*. Elijah means *the Lord God*. Warner means *defender*. "Lord Jesus, let Caiden be a valiant war-

rior and defender of the Lord my God!" To this very day, I remind Caiden of the powerful God-given significance of his name.

I believe children often reflect the meaning of their name. A fun example happened when we met up with my son, daughter-in-law, and their two children at a huge warehouse club. My grandson, Caiden, at four years of age, is full of energy. There was no way he wasn't going exploring in the huge store, so I suggested he and I go over to Party City while Gramps, Mommy, Daddy, and one-year-old Gracelyn shopped.

In Party City, Caiden declared, "Grammy, I want a superhero costume." As with any good grammy, my immediate answer was, "Yes!" I want my grandson to know that God, His heavenly Father, wants to lavishly pour out gifts on him. So I, Grammy, as often as I can, will be generous. Caiden led me to the costumes. He decided he wanted a Spider-Man® costume. At home, he has hooks with a fireman's costume, a Batman® costume, a dark elevator (Darth Vader®) costume, a Superman® costume, a policeman costume, and more. So now we added a Spider-Man® costume.

Caiden immediately started to put it on so he could go show Mommy. When we arrived back at the big store, we saw some little boys whose eyes got so big as my pint-size Spider-Man® walked by them. Caiden walked proudly. Then he spotted Mommy, Daddy and Gramps at the other end of the store. He took off running the full length of the store. He was so excited! He not only looked like a superhero, but also felt like a superhero. He even shot pretend webs to tie up Gramps. For that moment in time, Caiden was Spider-Man®.

How does that relate to the meaning of Caiden's name—Valiant Warrior and Defender of the Lord my God? As a young child he is already becoming who God created him to be—a SUPERHERO for the kingdom of God! I don't know what his true calling is yet, but I do know he is already developing into a Valiant Warrior and Defender of the Lord my God, cape and all.

My Aunt Grace told me that her mother (my grandmother) Ruth always had a victorious spirit. She had a prayer closet. Even if she went into the prayer closet with tears flowing, she always came out in peace with total contentment. God always gave her the answer in the closet. Aunt Grace, now in her 70's, still recalls vividly the power of the closet.

Aunt Grace remembered when her mom was praying for the rent money. Grandma needed $32.50 for the rent. She opened an unmarked envelope. Inside there was $35. During another time of need, they found a sack of groceries on their porch. When Grace brought a need to Grandma, Grandma immediately prayed and knew that God would take care of her. Grandma had total faith in her supernatural Father.

During Aunt Grace's wayward days, one time when she came home, her mom asked, "Where were you last night. You were in grave danger. My prayers protected your life." Even though Grace lied about where she had been, she knew exactly what her mom was talking about.

Again and again as I interviewed my Aunt Grace, she told me about the God stories her mom shared with her. From the youngest age, Aunt Grace had no doubt that God was real because of the amazing miracles she heard her mom tell. When Grandma was in an accident, she laughed at how the angels protected the car. When she had a flat tire, God was there. When she was in a gang violent area, she felt surrounded by angels. She was not afraid to travel across the country alone at seventy-five years of age. (She drove three thousand miles alone to attend my high school graduation.)

God was her divine protector. No fear. She forgot her purse, drove back four hours to the place, and found the purse untouched with all money intact. Aunt Grace told me that God was so real in her house because her mom found power in the prayer closet. Aunt Grace learned from a young age how to spend precious time in her closet to live victoriously through a difficult marriage.

When I was seven years old, we moved to Massena, New York, where my dad took a new pastorate. He was warned how difficult a place it was to pastor, but he followed the leading of the Lord as he went. The first summer, Mom and Dad jumped full force into ministry by putting together a two-week long Vacation Bible School for the children. My dad was excellent at this kind of ministry, which attracted lots of children from all over the community. During the first week, not one child responded to the altar calls. This was quite unusual because children's hearts are typically very sensitive to the Spirit.

During that first week, my mom had a dream about my older brother coming in the back door with his hands covering his face. His eye was hanging out of the socket and badly bleeding. My parents immediately began to pray. Later that day, my brother Dan came in the back door with his hands covering his face in the same way as in the dream, but instead of his eye hanging out, there were only scratches on his face. He said that a branch came down while he was walking through the woods and scratched his face. God quickly answered my parents' prayer.

But the battle was not over. The next day, I was riding my new bicycle down the hill when my chain came off. Instead of turning, in a panic I hit the curb and ended up with fifteen stitches in the back of my leg. The day after that, my brother David was walking into the bedroom when the door slammed into his face and broke his front tooth.

My dad said, he felt like the enemy was against him and that he should just take his whole family, put them in the car, and get out of there before something worse happened. But, he knew that God was the answer. He gathered our family together and we prayed until we had **prayed through**. All attacks against our family stopped!

There were immediate positive results. The second week of Vacation Bible School, more children accepted Christ as their personal Savior than the church had ever seen before. God was victorious! And of course, praying with dad and mom showed us kids how powerful our God is!

What about the generational inheritance that we pass on to our children? What credentials have we earned that we want them to carry? What ground have we gained that we want them to hold? More than that, how do we position them to go farther with God than we ever could? As children, hopefully our kids follow the God of mom and dad. But eventually they must choose for themselves. The old song reminds us, "I have decided to follow Jesus." The God of Abraham, Isaac, and Jacob, the God of mom and dad, must become the personal God of my son and daughter. My love and passion for God can only carry them so far.

Constant prayer, consistent prayer, fervent prayer is a key. When my sons were at school I would often go into their bedrooms and pray for them. In addition to prayer, having family devotions, teaching our children to pray for specific needs, sharing as God answers prayer, encouraging them to memorize Scripture, modeling to our children our love for God, and communicating what we are experiencing as we grow in Christ are a few ways to prime their spiritual pump.

Sometimes our children see God in how we handle grief and loss.

In the 1980s, we planted a church in East Aurora, New York. We had seven great years of ministry. We poured out our blood, sweat, and tears as we grew a congregation that we deeply loved and who loved us. It wasn't all easy. In a roofing accident, Al severely fractured his ankle. Later on, Al had surgery for a stomach issue that went horribly wrong. Still, we loved our church family and felt their love through all this.

As we began to embrace our Pentecostal inheritance, our lives were turned upside down. God was calling us out of the pastorate to a non-traditional ministry. Our whole family felt the pain of leaving behind the familiar, our church family, for the unknown. Our sons especially felt the pain as they said goodbye to their friends and to the school they loved. We prayed for them as they tried to adjust to a new life where their dad was not their pastor. There were a lot of bumps in the road for us all.

We spent the next few years wondering what God was calling us to do. We felt strongly that we were called to bring the Body of Christ together across racial and denominational lines. We knew somehow that it would include pastors, business leaders, government leaders, and educators, but we didn't know what it would look like or how we were supposed to make this happen. As we prayed, God gave us a strategy to be spies in the land. We needed to know what God was up to all around Western New York.

For a season, each Sunday, our family would attend a different church. We wanted to experience together this new call to see the Body of Christ come together. One Sunday, we attended a Lutheran Church with closed communion, liturgy, incense, and robes. The next Sunday, we attended a Church of God in Christ Church where they danced in the aisles and the service lasted three hours. Our sons watched, sometimes wide-eyed, but they developed a well-rounded view of God. Our prayers covered them during the transition, hoping they would catch how big and diverse God really is.

We believed we had been faithful to do what we had been called to do in the past that included our time in a rural church in Upstate New York, a Puerto Rican church in Chicago, a Chinese church in Hong Kong, and an upscale suburban church in East Aurora, but it appeared the puzzle box had really gotten shaken up this time as we experienced churches all over the City of Buffalo. In many ways, we felt like we were starting from scratch again. We were both working secular jobs and yet believed God's call was still upon us for full-time ministry.

In 1997, Set Free Inc., our non-profit, finally began to take shape. It fit the bill of building bridges between leaders to transform their world. We worked with leaders across racial and denominational lines, yet we still felt like something was missing. We believed the Scripture,

"Don't be misled—you cannot mock the justice of God. You will always harvest what you plant. Those who live only to satisfy their own sinful nature will harvest decay and death from that sinful nature. But those who live to please the Spirit will harvest everlasting life from the Spirit. So let's not get tired of doing what is good. At just the right time we will reap a harvest of blessing if we don't give up" (Galatians 6:7-9 NLT).

John Paul Jackson gave us the missing piece in a powerful teaching. His wife was in a horrible car accident. Insurance paid the medical bills, but she also received much more money for her pain and suffering. John Paul suggested that we should seek God to pay us back for pain and suffering that we had experienced in our Kingdom assignment.

For some reason, this hit home with us. We did a crazy thing. We drove to East Aurora to our old church parking lot. We remembered Al's surgeries. We remembered other "war wounds" we had experienced, some of which were still with us. We had sowed into the soil of East Aurora with our very own lives believing for a great church to arise. But things hadn't gone the way we thought they would.

So we sat there in our car and began to pray. We asked for forgiveness for anytime we missed the mark. We prayed against any spirit of hope deferred that we were carrying. We prayed and blessed people in the congregation, even those who had left. We prayed that where we sowed good seeds, we would now reap a good harvest. We prayed that for all the pain and suffering, we would receive a good harvest. With God it is about the journey, not just the destination, so we believed we qualified for a return on our investment that would be released into our new ministry assignment.

After this prayer time, we felt a burden lift. We were amazed as the money that we needed for the next steps in our ministry began to be released in unusual ways. God gave us creative strategies to begin to fund the needs of our non-traditional ministry, Set Free.

This didn't happen overnight, but we knew our sons were watching our step of faith. Like us, they were unsure of where the money was going to come from. But where God guides, He always provides. There has always been enough. Every bill has been paid, every need met. May our children witness the supernatural provision of God and testify to what a great and loving Father He is!

My sons may never read this book (if either of you reads this sentence, please let me know!), that's reality.... But they know that their mother and father have prayed for them. We've modeled for them time spent with the Father in the closet. Until the day we die, we will continue to remind our family of the many answers to prayer we have witnessed.

We will continue to tell them about the favor of God that surrounds them. We will remind them of their strong spiritual inheritance. We will talk about the overcomers and entrepreneurs in our family tree. We will talk about the saints (and a little bit about the sinners) in our family tree. We will remind them that they stand on strong generational shoulders of those who have gone before. Our prayer will always be that they too will experience "the incredible greatness of God's power for us who believe

Him" (Eph. 1:19 NLT). **Our prayers will bear fruit for generations to come and so will yours!**

In order to pass down your generational inheritance successfully, use the keys God has given you, including praying and prophesying life. I love to step into an anointed song to launch higher.

Currently the song, "The Blessing," by Kari Jobe, is an example of singing blessing over our family and the generations to come. Join with me in singing this over both your family and generations yet to be born.

> *The Lord bless you*
> *And keep you*
> *Make His face shine upon you*
> *And be gracious to you*
> *The Lord turn His*
> *Face toward you*
> *And give you peace*
> *Amen, amen, amen*
> *As we receive, we agree, amen, amen, amen, amen*
> ***May His favor be upon you***
> ***And a thousand generations***
> ***And your family and your children***
> ***And their children***
> ***And their children …***

Chapter 21

Your Treasure

To RECAP, SCARECROWS, BONES, CLOSETS, HUGS, FUNERALS, God sightings—
they are all puzzle pieces. Assembling experiences and memories is like
looking at the topside of a quilt. It takes a while, but eventually the pattern
starts to come together.

Funny, after all these years, I still have more puzzle pieces in my hand
than I know what to do with. What about you? Have I encouraged you to
put your puzzle together? Or are you still wondering where to start? Are
there generational inheritance puzzle pieces that you have never embraced?
Have you thought of the family you have in heaven who are cheering you
on to find and put together those long-lost pieces so the pattern can emerge
and the treasure can be revealed?

Do you have family members who are still here who you can ask mean-
ingful questions? Are there scarecrows that you need to face down in order
to find the hidden treasure buried beneath them? As you have read these
chapters, has God revealed to you hidden keys that you haven't explored
yet? Are their prophetic words that have been spoken over you that still lay
dormant and unrealized?

What is the goal in recovering a generational inheritance?

• Is it just to be a student of history to unlock the past?

- Is it to motivate you to push forward to fulfill the calling of God on your life?
- Is it to stand taller, understanding the call of God on you within your specific family?
- Is it about the kingdom of God causing everything to work together as you love and follow Him?

"Therefore, since we are surrounded by such a huge crowd of witnesses to the life of faith, **let us strip off every weight that slows us down**, especially the sin that so easily trips us up. And let us run with endurance the race God has set before us. We do this by keeping our eyes on Jesus, the champion who initiates and perfects our faith. Because of the joy awaiting him, he endured the cross, disregarding its shame. Now he is seated in the place of honor beside God's throne. Think of all the hostility he endured from sinful people; then you won't become weary and give up. After all, you have not yet given your lives in your struggle against sin" (Hebrews 12:1-4 NLT).

Maybe you are still struggling with some personal scarecrows that seem larger than life. How will you deal with them? Let me encourage you that there is great freedom available to you as you come closer into the Father's loving arms.

Years ago, because of wounds from my childhood, I was afraid of everything. The thought of standing in front of a room to speak caused my mouth to completely dry up. I was totally afraid of the dark. I used a nightlight as a child to keep my fear at bay, but as I grew older I was known to sing, "Alleluia!" at the top of my lungs when I had to go outside in the dark. I was completely intimidated by men or by anyone in authority. I memorized the verse from Philippians 4:13 (KJV): "I can do all things through Christ who strengthens me."

I quoted that verse over and over and over to myself growing up just to get through simple tasks. I truly believed I was overcoming my fears by these coping skills I had developed. I thought this would be my forever normal. I didn't understand that true freedom was available.

But there came the day when my trials were too much. Our marriage was struggling. The church we pastored was going through its own turmoil. Extended family relationships were at an all time low. I became desperate. I went for help. A simple prayer with trusted friends walked me through a personal deliverance that changed me forever. I didn't even know such freedom was available in Christ. There were new behaviors I had to learn to walk in to maintain and establish my freedom, but I was never the same again.

You have more cheerleaders than you know, both living and dead. Heroes of the faith stand alongside family members rooting you on so that nothing will be lost, everything will be recovered. They want you to run faster and climb higher than they did. Most of all, they want you to finish well. From their viewpoint, they see the bigger picture from eternity past through eternity future. They are no longer looking from the view of the penguin, but have an eagle eye from above. They see the Kingdom from a totally different perspective. They want you to come up higher in your thought and prayer life. They want you to recognize the champion call that is on your life. They want to raise your dreams beyond your wildest dreams. They want you to reach higher than they ever dared. They want to release a confidence to you about who you are in Christ so that you can endure whatever trial or temptation or distraction you face in order to go the distance to win the race set before you.

Theses heroes of the faith looking on from heaven have already paid a heavy price. They may have interceded for hours for you specifically. They may have fought battles on your behalf that you don't even know about. They may have given up much to give to you a deeper understanding of God's Kingdom at work in you. They know their efforts were not wasted.

They sowed into you expecting God to give you a holy harvest. It's your turn. The baton is available to you. This baton carries the blood, sweat, and tears of generations that have gone before you. Run your lap well before you pass the baton to the next generation.

2 Kings 13:21 (NLT) tells the story of a dead man who was thrown into Elisha's tomb to hide him, but the results were startling: "Once when some Israelites were burying a man, they spied a band of these raiders. So they hastily threw the corpse into the tomb of Elisha and fled. But as soon as the body touched Elisha's bones, the dead man revived and jumped to his feet!"

Even Elisha's dead bones carried one more miracle—Resurrection! Could there still be life in the family bones that were buried years before you were even born? Dig up the stories you're your family's past. Pray over your inheritance, and study the hidden treasures your family left behind. Maybe you will find a life-changing treasure as I did as I dug through my family history. Join me as a treasure hunter, shoulder to shoulder, recovering all your generational inheritance and claiming the treasure that belongs to you!

Thank you for journeying with me. My journey is not finished, and neither is yours. God is still revealing new treasures each day of our lives, as he continues to help put puzzle pieces together. I may have more journeys to take to recover more of my spiritual inheritance. Only God knows the future.

As we close, please pray this prayer with me:

Heavenly Father, I sit here with puzzle pieces piled high around me, knowing I will find still more as I press forward. God, go before me and order my steps that I might identify, clean off, and carefully put together my family history to redeem my family inheritance.

Breathe life on the powerful seeds that were planted years ago by past family members. Help me to see and destroy the

scarecrows in my past that have kept me from my full potential. Uncover my spiritual inheritance that I may walk in the earned credentials of my family as a world changer to see Your Kingdom arise.

I choose to pick up and run with the baton in my hands. I want to effectively run my leg of the race and prepare the way for the next generation to grab the baton and win the leg set before them.

In Jesus' Name AMEN!

Appendix

Telling the Lord's Secrets:
The Story of Daniel Awrey

By Glenn Gohr

ALTHOUGH MUCH FANFARE HAS BEEN DEVOTED TO commemorating the 100th anniversary of the Pentecostal outpouring which occurred at Topeka, Kansas, on January 1, 1901, that is not the only watchnight service where God poured out his Spirit in the early days. Another important incident of Holy Spirit baptism occurred 10 years to the day prior to the Topeka revival. Daniel Awrey, who is considered a pivotal figure in early Pentecost, received the baptism of the Holy Spirit on January 1, 1891 at Delaware, Ohio.

Awrey was a traveling holiness preacher who later went as a missionary to India, Hong Kong, South America, and to Liberia, where he died in service to the gospel. He published a number of tracts, and in a series of articles printed in *The Latter Rain Evangel*, a publication of the Stone Church in Chicago, he gave his life story. The report of his Spirit baptism is briefly mentioned in a number of Pentecostal reference works, including B. F. Lawrence's *The Apostolic Faith Restored* and Stanley Frodsham's *With Signs Following*. Further references to Awrey are found in early periodicals such as *Live Coals of Fire*, the *Way of Faith*, *Triumphs of Faith*, *Confidence*, and the *Christian Evangel*. It is obvious that Daniel Awrey made an outstanding contribution to the Pentecostal movement which should not be overlooked.

Daniel Awrey was born on February 10, 1869 at Mimosa, Ontario, Canada.[1] He was one of twelve children and came from Irish-German stock. His parents were godly people who had family prayer and took their family to church as often as possible. At about age 16 he went to the altar to seek salvation and wept bitterly. This was a turning point in his life because it caused him to think deeply about the things of God. At this point he believed he was a Christian, but yet something wasn't quite right.

In October 1887, Awrey began a three years' contract to learn the milling trade in Hawley, Minnesota. Then one night, a little before sundown, Awrey went to oil the dangerous places in the machinery at the mill. The floor was wet, and when he reached the highest point to oil some bearings, he lost his footing and nearly went headlong into some great cogwheels about ten feet below. He threw his hand against a running shaft and pushed himself back. In the meantime, it seemed that his whole life flashed in front of him. A piece of red machinery about 20 feet below him became as the lake of fire in his mind's eye, and he realized that he still had unforgiven sin in his life. He repented, and from that point on he was not satisfied to just attend church and be what some might call a nominal Christian, he wanted to *know* the Lord.

His pastor in 1889 was H. W. Sanderson of Ohio, who was a very spiritual man and who greatly influenced him. Sanderson gave him a book about the life of a converted Catholic which caused Awrey to want some assurance that he truly was saved.[1a]

On the night of March 6, 1890, Awrey prayed in his room, dropped to his knees, asked for forgiveness,and committed his life to God in the name of Jesus. This time he was filled with love, joy and peace and felt the assurance that he was saved.[2]

The next morning he started the day with prayer. On the way to work he began to sing "Safe in the Arms of Jesus." And that day it seemed as if the mill ran smoother and better than ever. He told everybody how he felt, and he was soon called crazy by some, but it was the happiest kind of craziness he had ever known.

A few months later, while visiting in St. Paul and Minneapolis, he saw a great need for people to hear the gospel. There was work to be done. As he prayed, he felt the Lord speak to him, "Go, preach My gospel." At first Awrey made excuses to God. Then he told God, "If you can do anything with me, I will go."

Returning to Hawley, he was encouraged by his pastor and did some exhorting and began to lead singing. In December of 1890, Awrey started attending a college at Delaware, Ohio, arriving there on December 24th.[2a] He stayed with Pastor Samuelson's father and began reading a book called *Perfect Love* by J. A. Wood which described the Christian experience in such a way that it caused Awrey to seek more from God.

On the last night of the old year of 1890, Awrey was reading in the this book until about quarter to twelve. Having decided to start the New Year on his knees, he laid down the book, and then he felt the Lord speak to his heart, "There is another experience for you."

Meditating further on what he had read in the book and what he knew to be true from the Scriptures, Awrey was ready for whatever the Lord had in store for him. He told God, "If there is, I am going to have it, and I am going to kneel down her for it, and I will never get up without it." He expected to be there for several hours.

When the whistles began to blow and the bells rang out announcing the New Year, he dropped to his knees and believed and trusted in God to sanctify him wholly in every way possible. A real peace flooded his soul.

The next morning while conducting family worship in the Samuelson home, he felt the anointing of the Holy Spirit in a powerful way. It was like oil being poured throughout his spirit, soul, and body.

That night, the first night of the new year, he went to prayer meeting, and after calling on several others to pray, the leader asked for voluntary prayer. Awrey reports, "I began to pray and the Holy Spirit prayed through me in another tongue, and by faith the prayer went right up to the throne of God."[3] He says that he saw a flame of fire come down on his head and the Lord took control of his tongue, making him pray in another language.[4] The blessing of God went all through his being. He felt like all three persons of the Trinity had come to dwell in his heart and life in a very real way.

Preaching the Gospel

Awrey remained at the college until spring and then returned to his old home at Mimosa, Ontario, where he began testifying and holding services. In June 1891 he felt prompted to attend some tent meetings at Grand Rapids, Michigan. He only had enough money to stay for two weeks, but then he got a job taking care of the tent at night, so he stayed for three months.

The tent being idle for awhile, Awrey and two others went to another part of the city and began a meeting. Awrey had led a few meetings, but he had never really preached before. He reports, "I prayed, found a text in the Bible, read some books and soon felt I could preach for an hour without any trouble."[5]

But once the tent was full of people, and the time came for the sermon, Awrey says, "I got up, and in about five minutes I said all I could think of, and there I stood. I looked at the people and they looked at me." It seemed the devil was telling him that he had made a fool of himself and that he should sit down. But Awrey refused. He prayed for help and it came.

"The power came upon me so that I could hardly stand up," declared Awrey. "I began to relate some of my experiences and as I talked the tears came to my eyes; the people also began to weep, till the whole congregation were weeping." When he gave the invitation that twenty-four-foot altar was filled with people. Several were saved, and Awrey was encouraged.[6]

From Grand Rapids, Awrey held meetings in Ransom, Michigan, at the invitation of H. W. Sanderson, and in other towns in Michigan and Ohio.

While living and working in the mill at Hawley, Minnesota, he became acquainted with Ella Olson Braseth, a native of Norway, who was working in the house where he lived. After being saved, Awrey testified at the table of what the Lord had done for him. Soon the Spirit began to convict her, and she asked him to pray for her, which he did. She was saved in September 1890, and on March 25, 1893 they were married at Fargo, North Dakota.[7] Shortly afterwards they went to Tennessee where Awrey began evangelizing in a number of different communities.

Struggles and Persecution

He went everywhere preaching the gospel and holy living according to the Bible standard, and many did not like it. He was ordered away from many places and told that he was not welcome. He didn't get any money at these services he was holding.

After several weeks it seemed the Lord was saying to him, "Do you expect to go on this way?" He replied, "Yes, Lord, if I starve to death." He gladly would have worked, but he could find no work to do. Then in November he had a chance to help out with the corn harvest and worked a few days in the coal mines. Still the devil would tempt him many times for leaving a good trade and preaching for nothing.

Awrey and his wife especially found it hard making ends meet after their first baby arrived on January 2, 1894. Soon all their money was gone, and they had no food in the house. Ella looked at her husband and said, "What are we going to do for dinner?" Awrey replied, "We are going to trust the Lord."

"Yes," she said, "of course, we are going to trust the Lord, but what are we going to do for dinner?" He went to the post office, but was not expecting anything. Name after name was called out for those to receive mail. The devil kept telling Awrey, "There is nothing for you." But the very last name called was his, and the letter contained seven dollars. He began to shout and praise God right there in the post office. A tall man looking over his shoulder said, "Well, you have something to shout over this morning." He was able to purchase some food, and that noon they were able to have a splendid dinner.

On March 25th, he started out on a missionary trip, holding meetings in various towns and hamlets in Kentucky and Tennessee. For part of this time he was assisting a cousin who was on a circuit in the Cumberland Mountains. He ended the year holding meetings at Tarlton and Beersheba Springs, Tennessee. In nine months' time he had traveled over a thousand miles on foot, and his offerings, together with what he earned in the coal mines during that time only amounted to forty dollars and thirty cents.[8]

On January 19, 1895, he was ordained in the Congregational Methodist Church.[9] At the same time, Awrey reports that he received some wonderful promises for the outpouring of God's Spirit. He went up into the mountains, secured a schoolhouse and later a vacant house, and began holding services. He preached a strong message of holiness and sanctification and more than 50 souls were claimed for God in those meetings.

He also had to contend with persecution. One time when he was holding meetings, God warned him with a scripture: "Up, get thee out of this place" (Genesis 19:14). The next night he decided to hold a meeting in a different place than where he had been preaching. That next night several men wearing white caps were hunting for him to do him harm. Fortunately he had been warned, and they could not locate him.

Another time Awrey felt the Lord telling him to go to Texas. He reported that God told him: "I have many people on the way who need the truth, and I want you to walk. Will you go?" Awrey's reply was "Yes, Lord." Soon

Awrey's cousin (having no knowledge of what the Lord had spoken to Awrey) came and proposed that they go to Texas. The cousin had money, but in keeping with what the Lord had shown him, he said, "If you will walk I will go with you." The cousin agreed. Walking about 30 miles a day, the ate blackberries and plums which grew along the roadside. They would walk at night, sleep during the day, and preach on Sundays.

While on their journey, the Lord frequently gave Awrey the assurance that people whom he met and spoke with would be saved. When Awrey reached Shreveport, Louisiana, he bought some clothes with money he had received from meager offerings and from a few odd jobs he had worked along the way. He held services there, and with the money he received in the offering, he was able to take a train to Marshall, Texas. While in Texas, he participated in a number of camp meetings. At Doddridge, Texas, a collection was received that enabled him to bring his wife and family to Texas.

Awrey traveled throughout eastern and northern Texas holding meetings from place to place. At the close of 1895 he had logged in over a thousand miles on foot and only received $64.65 in offerings.[10]

The next spring he ministered at Springdale, Texas, and many prayers were answered. Awrey prayed that such mighty conviction might come on the people that they could not sleep, and if nothing else would move them, that there might be a cyclone.

The next day, after praying that prayer, it rained all day, and at night the wind changed and a fierce-looking cloud came from the west. The people saw it and said, "There comes the cyclone." Being brought under conviction, a number of people prayed for God's mercy and were saved.

Another night four young men came to the altar, but the Lord showed Awrey that they had not come for any good purpose. Instead of instructing them on how to be saved, he warned them to "flee from the wrath to come." Three of them got up an left and went to a dance the next night. All three became sick and died within 3 weeks' time. The fourth young man was in a bad accident with a carriage and was almost trampled by the horse. He called out to God for one more chance. He was saved from sin, and his life was spared.

A schoolteacher at Springdale was also healed of a twitching in her eyes, no longer had to wear glasses, and could read fine print after prayer was offered in her behalf.

Beaten With Many Stripes

From Springdale, Awrey moved to Atlanta, Texas. He held a meeting in a schoolhouse at nearby O'Farrell where about 15 were saved. But some evil reports began to spread, and one man threatened to run him out of town. A few days later, as he was returning from the post office, a man ran up and said, "When are you going to leave this town?" Awrey told him that he lived there and did not intend to leave.

With that, the man grabbed an old board left over from a picket fence and broke it over Awrey's head. He took other boards and beat him about the shoulders and back. Then he knocked Awrey's head against a telephone pole.

A prayer arose in Awrey's heart, "Father forgive him, for he knows not what he does." The man proceeded to hit him with a stick, and by this time a crowd had gathered. An old blacksmith went to get his gun, and the assailant fled.

During the time of the beating, Awrey had not uttered a word. Once the ordeal was over, he praised and shouted "Glory to God" for protecting him. Awrey reports that the Lord kept him in such perfect peace and so filled with love, that he didn't even feel any pain in his body.[11]

Afterwards the mayor called on him, and Awrey had the opportunity to share what great things the Lord had done for him. The man who had assaulted him was fined $17.00. Later the man learned that the report he had heard, which had caused the beating, was untrue. Awrey tried to make friends, but the man refused.

Another time, after coming home from prayer meeting he heard a rap at the door. Awrey sensed that someone meant him harm. He looked out and saw a man with a large club under his coat. He said he wanted Awrey to visit a sick family and pray with them. Awrey replied that he was no doctor and shut the door. The man came back again, this time with a mob. He said that Awrey just had to come. In answer, he said he would go in the morning. Then Awrey and his family sneaked over to the mayor's house and stayed there all night.

On July 4, 1896, some men with pistols threatened to kill him. They took him to the railroad track and asked if he wanted to be hung to a telegraph pole or to be whipped. The men cut some switches and began to beat his bare back. They made several propositions to him, but he would not agree, so they continued to strike him unmercifully. Afterwards, without malice he preached to them under the power of the Spirit and said, "Goodbye, we will meet at the judgment." Although his back was raw, and a friend wrote a letter to the authorities that Awrey "was the worst treated white man he had ever seen," he was so full of God that he hardly felt any pain.

The newspapers reported, "The charge preferred against him is that he preaches the sanctification doctrine, and it was leading their friends astray."[12]

As Awrey prayed about this incident and other similar times of testing, several scriptures came to mind, including, "But when they persecute you in this city, flee ye into another" (Matthew 10:23). It was time to move on.

Trusting God for Divine Healing

Not long after this experience, the Awrey's baby became ill. They chose not to call on a physician, but instead anointed the child with oil. The fever immediately left him, but he was still weak. A neighbor woman came in, and when she discovered they were not using medicine, she became quite disturbed and went out and told others. After she left, they prayed again and the baby was perfectly well.

That Sunday the preacher, who had heard of the situation, was prepared to talk about fanaticism. The ministered floundered for awhile and finally denounced Awrey's "fanaticism." But Awrey was so happy that he could scarcely keep from shouting. He became the talk of the town, and several were saved from this incident. Many other incidents of healing are reported in Awrey's life testimony and in various testimonies published in early Pentecostal papers.

God's Provision

Shortly after his experience in Texas with the mob, he received an invitation to go to Arkansas to conduct meetings. In one place he witnessed to a known atheist, and that man and his family were all saved along with about fifty others. At Morris, Arkansas, he preached for about two weeks and over eighty were saved. He preached in several other places in Arkansas and Texas. At the end of 1896 he reported that 250 had been saved in his meetings.[13]

In 1897 he preached in Denton, Waco, Dublin, Red Point, Tyson, and other places in Texas. He continued on to Iowa Park and Canyon, Texas, in 1898, where large numbers were saved, and the Lord met his needs as he continued to live by faith.

One day while at Canyon, Awrey reported the Lord spoke to him and said: "You have followed Me everywhere I have asked you to go, in neglected and out-of-the way places where you did not get much, without drawing back or shrinking, but I have a wider field for you. In a day or two I want you to go to Minnesota." That was about 1400 miles away, and Awrey only had twenty cents. Awrey did some plowing for a week at Amarillo, Texas. Then some offerings came in from Iowa Park, Minnesota, and other places. Pretty soon he had a new suit of clothes and enough money to take his family to Hawley, Minnesota where he ministered for awhile.[14]

Several other incidents are recorded where God honored Awrey's faith by providing money or food when he was in impossible situations. Awrey had great faith and testified many times of the wonderful provision of God.

The World as His Mission Field

Daniel Awrey was a founding member of the Fire Baptized Holiness Association (FBHA) when it organized at Anderson, South Carolina, in July of 1898. In 1899 he was called the "Ruling Elder" of the FBHA in Tennessee, making his home at Beniah, Tennessee.[15] About a dozen people received the baptism of the Holy Spirit at Beniah in a widely publicized set of meetings held in 1899-1900, including his wife.[15a] This was a pivotal point in the history of the Pentecostal Holiness Church which came out of the Fire-Baptized movement as B. H. Irwin, Sarah Smith, W. F. Bryant, J. H. King, and others passed through Beniah about this time.[15b] Early in 1900, the Fire-Baptized Holiness Association established a School of the Prophets in Beniah, Tennessee.

During 1899, it is reported that Awrey made a 7,100 mile evangelistic trip through 18 states and two provinces of Canada.[16] In the latter part of 1899 and the early part of 1900 he evangelized in various places in Tennessee and Kentucky. He reports participating in a meeting at Dare, Tennessee conducted by Sarah Smith where he says "the jumping, and dancing and shouting was wonderful" and people were getting "baptized with the Holy Ghost and fire and dynamite."[17]

Receiving word of the Azusa Street Revival while evangelizing in Dudleyville, Arizona, Awrey visited the outpouring at Los Angeles and was convinced that the Pentecostal blessings there matched up with his own experience of Spirit baptism 15 years previous.[18]

In 1906, the Beulah Holiness Bible School, also called Emmanuel's Bible School, was established at Doxey, Oklahoma. Daniel Awrey later served as principal from about 1908-1909. (See "A. B. and Dora Cox" in *Heritage*, summer 1995 which mentions Awrey and the school.) Beulah remained open until 1910. This school produced many members for the Assemblies of God and for the Pentecostal Holiness Church.

When he left Oklahoma, he felt God directing him to take the Pentecostal message around the world. Reportedly, the Lord asked him to go to the railway station with only 10 cents in his pocket as a test of his faith and trust in mighty God.[19] Through the providence of God, beginning in 1909 Awrey circled the globe, traveling to Scotland, India, Hong Kong, South America, and other places doing missionary work.

During 1909 and 1910, Daniel Awrey was serving as a missionary in Hong Kong, where he helped establish a Bible school at Canton, with Mok Li Chi as his interpreter.[20] And in October of that year he spoke at a missionary convention at the Stone Church in Chicago. One of his talks was "Telling the Lord's Secrets" which later was published in tract form and distributed widely.[21] Some of his other messages which were preached at the Stone Church have also been reprinted in tract form.[22]

Also in 1909 participated in a Pentecostal World Conference in Europe. He spoke at the Sunderland Convention in England In 1909, 1910, and 1911, where he reported on his missionary journeys and came into contact with a number of important Pentecostal figures. Awrey was one of the early proponents of cooperation among Pentecostals worldwide. He influenced men and women such as A. A. Boddy, A. H. Post, Cecil Polhill, A. G. Garr, Pandita Ramabai, Carrie Judd Montgomery, T. B. Barratt, and others.[23] During 1910 and 1911, he traveled with Frank Bartleman, a leader from the Azusa Street Revival. They ministered in China and in India where Awrey preached at the Mukti Mission.[24]

Ethel E. Goss in *The Winds of God* gave high marks to Daniel Awrey whom she heard preach at Eureka Springs, Arkansas in 1911: "Daniel Awrey was a world-famous Bible teacher, missionary and traveler.... He was a man of cultivation and charm, but in his trips around the world, he used little of the abundant offerings he received for himself. In order to save and give to others, he bought steerage tickets and arranged to forego hotels by sitting up in trains at night. By living austerely, with much fasting, he was able to send thousands of dollars through the years to missionaries who were suffering privations in the field."[25a]

Daniel Awrey passed away on December 4, 1913, while ministering to the missions in Liberia, West Africa. After landing at Cape Palmas, Liberia on October 10, 1913, he became sick with what was termed as the blackwater or African fever three weeks after he landed, and he never recovered. His widow and family were living in Los Angeles at the time.[25]

J. Roswell Flower, editor of the *Christian Evangel*, knew Awrey from times that he had spoken to the congregation in Indianapolis. Before leaving for Liberia, Awrey had left his family in Los Angeles and visited different assemblies en route for the Atlantic Ocean. He stopped off in Plainfield, Indiana on July 29, 1913, and delivered an address to the students of the Gibeah Bible School where Flower was assisting.[26]

Flower wrote an appreciation to Daniel Awrey, reporting that he was a man well known in the Pentecostal work on five different continents, having traveled around the world three times, ministering in thousands of places. "He was always free-spirited, pleasant and victorious, and even his enemies will acknowledge that he was never heard to speak in a slighting way of anyone, no matter what attitude they had taken toward him, but that he had a good word to say for nearly everybody."[27]

Even though Daniel Awrey was the only one who received the baptism of the Holy Spirit in Delaware, Ohio, on New Year's Day in 1891, his ministry and influence which followed left a lasting impact on the Pentecostal Movement. Certainly his contribution is far-reaching. He traveled all across the United States and parts of Canada spreading the full gospel message. Then he took the gospel with him as he traveled around the world three times, ministering in five different continents. He influenced not only leaders in the Assemblies of God such as J. Roswell and Alice

Reynolds Flower, but he impacted other notables such as Frank Bartleman, Howard Goss, A. A. Boddy, T. B. Barratt, B. H. Irwin, J. H. King, and many others.

Notes

1. Daniel Awrey, "Life Sketches," *The Latter Rain Evangel* 2:6 (March 1910), 19.

2. Ibid.

3. Ibid., 20.

4. Undoubtedly this is Ohio Wesleyan University, although the school has no record of Awrey attending.

5. Awrey, "Life Sketches," 21.

6. *The Apostolic Faith* (Los Angeles, CA) 1:2 (October 1906), 4.

7. Awrey, "Life Sketches," 21.

8. Ibid.

9. Ibid.

10. Ibid., 23.

11. Daniel Awrey, "Life Sketches: 'Beaten With Many Stripes,'" *The Latter Rain Evangel* 2:7 (April 1910), 16.

12. Ibid., 17.

13. Ibid.

14. Ibid., 18.

15. Daniel Awrey, "Life Sketches: 'My God Shall Supply All Your Needs'," *The Latter Rain Evangel* 2:8 (May 1910), 21.

16. Ibid., 22.

17. Joseph E. Campbell, *The Pentecostal Holiness Church, 1898-1948: Its Background and History* (Raleigh, NC: World Outlook Publications, 1981, c1951), 199; Harold D. Hunter, "Beniah at the Apostolic Crossroads: Little Noticed Crosscurrents of B. H. Irwin, Charles Fox Parham, Frank Sandford, A. J. Tomlinson (Society For Pentecostal Studies, 1996), 22.

18. B. F. Lawrence, *The Apostolic Faith Restored* (St. Louis, MO: Gospel Publishing House, 1916), 45.

19. For further information on the significance of Beniah, Tennessee, see Harold D. Hunter's "Beniah at the Apostolic Crossroads: Little Noticed Crosscurrents of B. H. Irwin, Charles Fox Parham, Frank Sandford, A. J. Tomlinson (Society For Pentecostal Studies, 1996).

20. "Daniel Awrey's Letter," *Live Coals of Fire* 1:7 (December 1, 1899), 5.

21. "Daniel Awrey's Letter," *Live Coals of Fire* 1:10 (January 12, 1900), 2.

22. *The Apostolic Faith* (Los Angeles, CA) 1:2 (October 1906), 4.

23. Paul L. Ferguson, "Personal Recollections: Old Beulah Colony (OK)." Handwritten manuscript, 12 May 1992, 2.

24. *Confidence* 3:11 (November 1910), 252.

25. Daniel Awrey, "Telling the Lord's Secrets," *The Latter Rain Evangel* 2:2 (November 1909), 2.

26. Some other tracts of Daniel Awrey include: "How God Develops Us," "Finest of the Wheat," Filled With His Will," and "Use and Misuse of Gifts."

27. Awrey spoke at the Pentecostal Conference in Sunderland, England in May 1909 and came into contact with many early Pentecostal leaders from around the world, in addition to those he met on his missionary travels. See reports of Awrey's involvement in the Sunderland convention in *Confidence*, May 1909, 115; June 1909; July 1909; August 1909; July 1910; and *Triumphs of Faith*, July 1909, 152-154.

28. Frank Bartleman, *Azusa Street: The Roots of Modern-day Pentecost*

(Plainfield, NJ: Logos, 1980), 147.

29. Ethel E. Goss, *The Winds of God: The Story of the Early Pentecostal Movement (1901-1914) in the Life of Howard A. Goss* (Hazelwood, MO: Word Aflame Press, 1977), 254.

30. *The Latter Rain Evangel* 6:5 (February 1914), 14.

31. "Daniel Awrey: His Home Call in West Africa," *Confidence* 7:2 (February 1914), 35-36. This tribute was originally published in the *Christian Evangel;* however, few copies of the *Evangel* from 1913 have survived.

32. Ibid., 35.

This article is reprinted by permission from *Assemblies of God Heritage* 20:4 (Winter 2000-01).

Sources For Further Research

Sources on Daniel Awrey

Awrey, Daniel. "Life Sketches," *Latter Rain Evangel,* March 1910, pp. 19-23.

Awrey, Daniel. "Life Sketches: My God Shall Supply All Your Needs," *Latter Rain Evangel,* May 1910, pp. 20-22.

Awrey, Daniel. *Telling the Lord's Secrets* [tract]. Los Angeles: Free Tract Society: A Call to Faith, n.d. 8 p.

"Awrey, Daniel P." In *New International Dictionary of Pentecostal and Charismatic Movements.* Stanley M. Burgess and Eduard M. van der Maas, eds. Rev. and expanded ed. Grand Rapids, MI: Zondervan, 2002. p. 344.

Gohr, Glenn. "Telling the Lord's Secrets: The Story of Daniel Awrey." *Assemblies of God Heritage* 20:4 (Winter 2000-01): 22-28.

Hunter, Harold D. "Beniah at the Apostolic Crossroads: Little Noticed Crosscurrents of B H Irwin, Charles Fox Parham, Frank Sandford, A J Tomlinson." *Cyberjournal for Pentecostal-Charismatic Research,* 1 Jan 1997.

Warner, Al. "Daniel Awrey: Azusa Street Itinerant Missionary Evangelist." Lakeland, FL: Society For Pentecostal Studies, March 2015.

Woods, Daniel. "Daniel Awrey, the Fire-Baptized Movement, and the Origins of the Church of God: Toward a Chronology of Confluence and Influence." *Cyberjournal for Pentecostal-Charismatic Research,* 19 Jan 2010.

Articles on Generational Inheritance

Brunson, Rick. "Discovering Your Spiritual Roots." *Charisma & Christian Life* (October 1995): 74-77.

Gohr, Glenn. "Spiritual Roots of the Flower Family." *Assemblies of God Heritage* 17:4 (Winter 1997-98): 7-11, 31.

Olena, Lois E. "Stanley M. Horton: A Pentecostal Journey." *Assemblies of God Heritage* 29 (2009): 4-14.

Warner, Wayne. "A Powerful Witness in New England: The Pentecostal Legacy of Clifford and Helen Crabtree." *Assemblies of God Heritage* 14: 2 (Summer 1994): 10-13, 27-29.

Books

Bartleman, Frank. *Azusa Street: The Roots of Modern-day Pentecost.* Plainfield, NJ: Logos, 1980.

Blumhofer, Edith. *Pentecost in My Soul: Explorations in the Meaning of Pentecostal Experience in the Assemblies of God.* Springfield, MO: Gospel Publishing House, 1989.

Cerullo, Morris. *Breaking and Reversing Generational Curses: How to Start Over with a Clean Slate.* San Diego, CA: Morris Cerullo World Evangelism, 2005.

Corum, Fred T., and Hazel E. Bakewell. *The Sparkling Fountain.* Windsor, Ohio: Corum & Associates, Inc., 1983.

Cunningham, Jewell Nicholson. *Covered Wagon Days of Evangelism.* N.p.: the author, 1990.

Esperance, Jarman. *The Twelve Spiritual Stones.* St. Petersburg, FL: Viking Communications, Inc., 1995.

Flower, Alice Reynolds. *Grace For Grace: Some Highlights of God's Grace in the Daily Life of the Flower Family.* Springfield, MO: the author, 1961.

Goss, Ethel E. *The Winds of God: The Story of the Early Pentecostal Movement (1901-1914) in the Life of Howard A. Goss.* Hazelwood, MO: Word Aflame Press, 1977.

Hickey, Marilyn. *Breaking Generational Curses: Overcoming the Legacy of Sin in Your Family*. Tulsa: Harrison House, 2000.

Hickey, Marilyn. *The Next Generation Blessings*. Denver, CO: Marilyn Hickey Ministries, 1995.

Hinn, Benny. *Kathryn Kuhlman: Her Spiritual Legacy and its Impact on my Life*. Nashville, TN: Thomas Nelson Publishers, 1999.

Morgan, Dan. *Rising in the West: The True Story of an Okie Family From the Great Depression Through the Reagan Years*. New York: Alfred A. Knopf, 1992.

Olena, Lois E., and Raymond L. Gannon. *Stanley M. Horton: Shaper of Pentecostal Theology*. Springfield, MO: Gospel Publishing House, 2009.

Peters, James. *Prevailing Westerlies (the Pentecostal Heritage of Maine): The Story of How the Pentecostal Fire Spread from Topeka, Kansas to Houston—to Los Angeles—to Bangor, Maine*. Shippensburg, PA: Destiny Image, c1988.

Pierce, Chuck D., and Rebecca Wagner Sytsema. *Possessing Your Inheritance: Moving Forward in God's Covenant Plan for Your life*. Ventura, CA : Renew, 1999.

Reid, Tommy, and Al Warner. *Create Wealth to Build God's Dream*. Clarence, NY: Kairos Publishing, 2015.

Reid, Tommy, and Al Warner. *Radical Revolution*. Strasburg, OH: Total Fusion Press, 2018.

Family History Research

America's Obituaries and Death Notices <https://www.newsbank.com>

Ancestry <www.ancestry.com>

Family Search <www.familysearch.org>

Fold3 History & Genealogy Archives <https://www.fold3.com/>

HeritageQuest® Online <https://www.proquest.com/products-services/HeritageQuest-Online.html>

National Archives and Records Administration <https://www.archives.gov/research>

Newspapers.com <www.newspapers.com.

The Statue of Liberty-Ellis Island Passenger Search <https://www.libertyellisfoundation.org/passenger>

Pentecostal Research

Apostolic Archives International, Inc. <https://www.apostolicarchives.com/>

Archives & Research Center, International Pentecostal Holiness Church <https://iphc.org/gso/archives/>

Archives & Special Collections, Asbury Theological Seminary <https://guides.asburyseminary.edu/archives>

Archives & Special Collections, Fuller Theological Seminary <https://digitalcommons.fuller.edu/archives/>

Consortium of Pentecostal Archives <pentecostalarchives.org>

Dixon Pentecostal Research Center <https://www.cogheritage.org/>

Flower Pentecostal Heritage Center <www.ifphc.org>

Foursquare Heritage Center <https://www.foursquare.org/about/history/heritage/>

Holy Spirit Research Center <https://digitalshowcase.oru.edu/hsrc/>

The Pentecostal Assemblies of Canada Archives <https://www.archeion.ca/pentecostal-assemblies-of-canada-archives>

Pentecostal Heritage Society, UPCI <http://upciheritage.faith/>

Special Collections & Archives, Regent University <https://www.regent.edu/lib/special-collections/home.cfm>

About the Author

DEB WARNER, ALONG WITH HER HUSBAND AL, are founders of Set Free, Inc., a networking ministry for building bridges between leaders to transform their world. This growing team of servant leaders in business, government, church, and education is working together to rebuild and transform the Buffalo/Niagara region. Deb and Al work consistently to bring the Body of Christ together across racial and denominational lines.

Deb and Al have over forty years of experience pastoring and equipping local churches and their leaders, including a term as missionaries to Hong Kong. Since 1999, they have facilitated a pastors prayer group in Buffalo. They invest their time encouraging and mentoring leaders to fulfill the call of God on their lives. Deb and Al preach and teach together—creating a Kingdom mindset. Deb loves to motivate and encourage people to be released as overcomers and world changers.

They have two adult sons: Caleb and Nathan, along with Nathan's wife, Megan, and grandchildren, Caiden, Gracelyn, and Emersyn.

For further information, visit www.setfreeleaders.com

CPSIA information can be obtained
at www.ICGtesting.com
Printed in the USA
FSHW020305060920
73440FS